Killer Mom : The True Story of Diane Downs

Barbara Daley

Published by Trellis Publishing, 2021.

KILLER MOM : THE TRUE STORY OF DIANE DOWNS

First edition. July 16, 2021.

Copyright © 2021 Barbara Daley.

ISBN: 979-8224297290

Written by Barbara Daley.

KILLER MOM : THE TRUE STORY OF DIANE DOWNS

1

BARBARA DALEY

At 22.48pm on May 19th, 1983, a young, single mother pulled up outside McKenzie-Willamette Hospital in Springfield, Oregon, in a blood-spattered Nissan Pulsar, repeatedly shouting that someone had shot her children. Hospital staff rushed to the car and found three children slumped inside. The mother, Diane Downs, had herself been shot in the left arm, which was wrapped in a blood-soaked towel.

As medics frantically tried to save the lives of the little ones, Diane told police that a man had flagged her down on the Old Mohawk Road, and demanded her car. When she had refused, he had leant into the car and shot her three children. According to Diane, she had struggled with the man who had then shot her in the arm. Pretending to throw the car keys into a field, she managed to distract the man long enough to get in her car and drive away, in a desperate bid to get the children to the hospital in time to save them. Tragically, 7-year-old Cheryl was already dead, and, although still alive, 3-year-old Danny and 8-year-old Christie were in a critical condition. The bone in Diane's arm was shattered.

While the people of Oregon, and the wider community, reeled in shock at this heinous crime and fearful of the bushy haired killer whom Diane had described, and who was still at large, the police were turning their attention to someone closer to home – the mother herself, Diane Downs.

Her Early Years
Diane was born Elizabeth Diane Frederickson in Phoenix, Arizona, on August 7th, 1955, to Wes and Willadene Frederickson. The oldest of four children, Diane lived a fairly nomadic life – moving from town to town with her parents and her younger siblings – John, Kathy, and Paul - until, at the age of 11, her father, Wes, found a steady position with the US Postal Service and the family at last put down some roots. Her mother, Willadene, also found a job with the US Postal Service, working as a clerk, at around the same time.

As a child, Diane (or Elizabeth as she was still known then) had a deep love for animals, as her father, Wes recalls:

"She had a couple of friends who had horses and she bugged us about buying her a horse until we finally gave in. I believe she was a freshman in high school at Moon Valley High School in Phoenix when we finally got her the horse. We lived in a subdivision in north-west Phoenix, in an area called Westtown and there was a stable less than a mile away from where she went daily to feed and care for the horse. Now there was a problem with having a horse, and that was, she didn't have enough time with the horse."1

It was this love of animals that led to yet another move for the Fredericksons, when the family spent a year living on a 10-acre farm in Phoenix.

"We always had a family session at evening meals. The standard meeting went like this: Diane talking about this and Diane talking about that. One day I said, "Diane, why don't you shut up and let someone else talk for a change". She shut up and sat there silent for about 3 minutes. There was nothing but sweet silence until Diane finally said: 'See! They didn't have anything to talk about.' At one of those evening meals, Diane brought up the issue about a farm. Everyone joined the cry except our oldest son. I remember at one of those family meetings, I made the statement, 'You don't want to move to a farm. There's all kinds of hardship. You have to work in the field. You have chores that you wouldn't have in the city. There are many hardships, more hardships than you would care to think about.' About that time, our youngest child, who was about three, raised his hand for recognition and said, 'Daddy, if you will buy me a sailor suit and a sailor hat, I'll go with you on your hardship.' That was the end of that meeting. The cry to buy a farm went on for weeks until we finally decided to give it a try. Another dumb move. So, for one year of our lives, we lived mostly on farms."1

Wes Frederickson recalls his decision to teach his children to hunt when his oldest child was a mere nine years of age.

"When Diane and the other children were young (I think Diane was about 9), I decided they needed to learn to hunt. Another dumb mistake. The prize of the day was 'dove'. I learned to hunt when I was young and I loved the taste of dove meat. We drove out west of Phoenix (we were living in Arizona) to Buckeye because that's one of the areas I used to hunt. We were having fun knocking around in the desert until I shot down the first dove and wounded it. I quickly removed its head and placed it in the bag to be eaten for supper. Diane screamed: 'No! Daddy! No!!' I didn't know it, but that was the end of the hunting trip. I would bring my shotgun up for a shot and Diane would scream, 'Miss! Miss!' Almost immediately there was a chorus of, 'Miss! Miss!' from all my children. Diane told me later that she wanted to bring that dove home and nurse it back to health." [1]

Her parents were devoted to their children but raised them without a lot of affection. Wes readily admits that he and his wife brought their children up to be strong, meaning they should not show any emotion, and indeed it was Diane's lack of emotion regarding the death of her daughter, and the trauma to her other children, which led to suspicions surrounding the shooting years later.

The Teenage Years

Up until the age of 14, Diane led what might be considered a 'sheltered' life. Influenced by her Baptist upbringing and strict parents, she was something of a misfit. With her parents not believing in following fashion or trends, Diane was out of touch and a bit of an 'oddball'. Something Diane has been quoted as saying might also suggest that she was a scapegoat at home. She claimed that she *"rarely babysat for her siblings because she hated it, being blamed for breakages and that she wasn't allowed to punish them."* [2]

At the age of 14, and tired of her conservative upbringing, Diane rebelled. She cut her 'childish' hair short, bleached it blond, and started wearing more fashionable clothes. It was also around this time that she dropped her first name, Elizabeth, and became known as Diane.

Along with this new interest in herself, came an awareness of boys. As her appearance became more provocative, so did her behavior and the interest shown in her by the opposite sex worked both ways.

When she was 15, a boy who lived across the street from the Fredericksons, 16-year-old Steven Downs, fell in love (or so he believed) with Diane, and by the time she was 16 their relationship was sexual. Her parents didn't like Steven and tried to discourage the relationship, but Diane didn't care, and the relationship continued.

Throughout these early teenage years, Diane remained an intelligent, conscientious student with a high IQ.

The relationship continued, and after graduation, Steven enlisted in the Navy, while Diane was sent to the Pacific Coast Baptist Bible College. However, a year later she was expelled for being promiscuous and sent back home to live with her parents. Despite her infidelity, the young couple continued their relationship and saw each other as often as possible, given the 30-mile distance between her parents' home in Phoenix, and Steven's in Chandler.

It was after one of her visits to see Steven in Chandler that Diane decided not to return home. Reportedly Wes, her father, was not happy with this and turned up at Steven's door with a shotgun and an ultimatum – *marry my daughter or else.*3

Steven and Diane

Steven and the then 19-year-old Diane, married on November 13th, 1973 and almost immediately the cracks began to show. Money was tight and Steven was working long hours, and, according to Diane, two weeks after their wedding Steven went on a date with another woman – arriving home in the early hours claiming his car had broken down.

Despite their problems, in 1974 Diane fell pregnant and in October of that year, Christie Ann Downs was born. Following the birth, Diane returned to her part-time job at a local store. However, when Steven was out of work and money was in short supply, the couple and their daughter had no choice but to move back in with Wes and Willadene.

Things were far from harmonious, and Diane has often claimed that everything Steven did was to be mean to her, just like her father.

When Christie was 6 months old, Diane enlisted in the Navy, but left after completing only three weeks of basic training – according to her, she had to get back to her baby as Steven was neglecting Christie in Diane's absence. By contrast, however, Steven claimed that Diane spent her time in training asking him to get her out of the Air Force or she would go AWOL. Either way, she was back home after less than a month.

1975 was an unhappy year for the couple, with Diane and Christie often running back to her parents' house (by this time the Downs' had their own home again). It has been suggested by Diane several times that it was Steven who sent them back home to her parents' house, and her parents who would send them back to Steven. Despite the problems, Diane became pregnant again and in January of 1976 their second child, Cheryl Lynn Downs was born.

After the birth of their second daughter, Steven decided he didn't want any more children and had a vasectomy. The operation failed, and Diane fell pregnant again. This time she opted for an abortion, and Steven had a second vasectomy.

October 1976 saw the family move to Flagstaff, Arizona, where Steven took two jobs to provide for his family. During this time Diane and the girls fled back to her parents several times after arguing with her husband. She claimed that during one of her stints back with her parents, the boss where she was working had raped her. It was a tumultuous time, and in 1978 they moved again, this time to Mesa, Arizona.

Both Steven and Diane began working for the same company, manufacturing mobile homes. It was while working on the assembly line there that Diane met and seduced a young co-worker by the name of Russ Phillips. When she found out she was pregnant, both Russ and Steven, who knew about the affair, urged her to have a termination, but Diane opted to continue with the pregnancy, and in December 1979 Stephen Daniel Downs was born. Even though Steven knew the baby wasn't his, he accepted him as his own.

It was also around the same time that Diane took a job at the Post Office. The only involvement that Russ Phillips allowed in his son's life was when Diane needed a babysitter, something which became more and more frequent.

As one of Diane's babysitters said *"If Danny wanted attention, Diane would push him away...but the worst thing was one time, I caught Cheryl jumping on the bed, and I said that was not permitted. I made her sit in a chair and think about it. Cheryl sat quietly for a while and then she looked up 'Do you have a gun here?' Of course not. Why? 'I want to shoot myself. My mom says I'm bad.' "*3 At that time, Cheryl would have been around three years old.

In 1980 the family moved back to Chandler, and Diane decided she wanted to become a surrogate mother, and started the process. She found yet another job, this time working as a letter carrier for the US Postal Service.

As part of the surrogacy process, Diane had to undergo psychiatric evaluations. The first psychiatrist to screen Diane referred her for more tests after deeming her 'neurotic'.

The report stated *"Diane did not do well in areas where she had to demonstrate social cause and effect reasoning, attention span and concept formation. These findings were consistent with, but not absolutely diagnostic, of a major psychopathology...The couple's last child, reportedly, was the result of Ms Downs' picking five "ugly" younger men to seduce in order to have a child by one of them....Ms. Downs's conversation was effusive, immature and frequently self-disparaging...This individual has poor ability to express anger in a modulated fashion and tends to have poor behavioral controls."*4

Despite the damning report, Diane underwent further evaluation in February 1981 in Phoenix with a different psychiatrist. He diagnosed her with a Histrionic Personality Disorder, but incredibly she was still approved as a candidate for the surrogacy program.

It was also around this time that the couple decided to divorce.

Diane, the Single Mother

Views surrounding Diane's abilities as a mother were conflicted. Sources close to Diane claim that she was a devoted mother who lived for her children. Neighbors, however, told a different story. In 1981, one of those neighbors, Mary Ward, wrote a letter to Diane, expressing concern about Cheryl's welfare. This incensed Diane, who showed up at her house denying the claims. According to Mary, Diane had told Cheryl *"You're such a bad little girl! If you don't obey Mommy, you deserve to be killed!"* Knowing that the children were often left alone, Mary Ward then offered to babysit the three children. *"Diane admitted she'd been abusive to her children but that she'd stopped shaking and screaming at them."*[4]

By this time, Diane was pregnant with a surrogate baby. She had flown to Kentucky and was successfully impregnated with the surrogate father's sperm, and in May 1982 Diane flew back to Kentucky to prepare for the birth.

After giving birth, and with the $10,000 she had been paid for the surrogacy, Diane returned home to Arizona and her own children, already vowing to repeat the experience. At this time, she was 25.

Friends and family used the surrogacy as proof of Diane's devotion to her children and desire to provide for them. There was even talk of opening her own surrogacy clinic, but those plans never came to fruition.

Neighbors continued to voice their concerns over Diane's three children. In a quote from the book *Small Sacrifices* by Anne Rule, the children's plight was noted.

"Diane had engaged in 'a pinch on the shoulder that left blue finger-marks, hair pulling, spanking, screaming at frightened little faces.'...'I'd usually grab them by the shoulders, scream, and make them sit down. They were quiet because they didn't know what mom would do. I pulled Cheryl's hair...I was in the bedroom. She saw the look on my face. She tried to run past me, and I grabbed for her shoulder...got her hair instead, and she fell on her little bottom...I was sorry later.' Cheryl always got the worst of it. 'If something broke, Cheryl broke it' Diane says, 'she was always hanging on something - or falling off something - or jumping on the furniture.'"

The Affairs

Diane was well known for her promiscuity, indulging in a multitude of affairs with men, most of whom were married. One man, in particular, caught her eye and they embarked on an affair which would eventually become the catalyst for the murder and attempted murder of her three children.

Robert 'Nick' Knickerbocker worked alongside Diane at the Post Office, and their dalliance quickly became something more, at least for Diane. She begged Nick to leave his wife, Nora, and be with her and the children but twice-married Nick wasn't so sure. One thing he was sure of, though, and made clear to Diane, was that he didn't want to be a father, either to a child of his own or to Diane's children. Such was his determination not to have children that he, like Steven, had had a vasectomy.

In September 1982, as Diane was scheduled for a second artificial insemination, she accused Nick of giving her a sexually transmitted disease. Nick denied this, knowing it couldn't be him as he had only been with Nora and Diane. By contrast, it was common knowledge that his mistress had been with at least four other men, and she was clearly the source of the infection.

Nick, in order to protect his wife, confessed to the affair. Nora, although devastated, agreed to give the marriage another try, and Nick ended his affair with Diane.

Diane returned to Kentucky for her insemination and firmly believed that Nora would end the marriage, clearing the way for her to be with the man she considered to be the love of her life. It was Steven, however, who was there to pick her up from the airport on her return from Kentucky, hoping to discuss a reconciliation between the two of them. Diane was disappointed when she saw Steven, thinking her lover would be there to pick her up, and the journey home was punctuated by anger and violence.

Steven claimed that he saw Diane put something black into her purse before running into her home and locking herself inside the bathroom, threatening suicide.

Steven, fearing for her life, broke down the door. Diane was inside, pointing the .22 pistol directly at him, and telling him that she couldn't kill herself but that she could kill him. Steven managed to calm Diane, and, taking the pistol with him, went home.

In November of 1982, Diane and the children moved back in with Steven, but life was far from idyllic. Nick's confession to his wife, Nora, had done nothing to ease Diane's obsession, and during a brief separation in the marriage, Diane started taunting Nora with phone calls, hanging up on her repeatedly. When that didn't work, Diane sent a letter to Nora telling her Nick was going to get a divorce. He wasn't, and he and Nora reconciled.

Nora's revenge came, though, when Diane's idea of opening a surrogacy clinic started to take shape, by telling the Kentucky clinic about both Diane's plans for her own clinic, and the sexually transmitted disease. This put paid to Diane's dreams of both opening her clinic, and of being a surrogate again, as her recent attempt at insemination had failed.

In April 1983, Diane and Nick's affair resumed, and Diane left for Oregon to start a new job, with Nick promising to follow. While helping Diane pack her things, Nick claimed that he saw a .38 pistol and a target pistol in the trunk of her car.

Once Diane had left, Nick was able to get his life in order, and he decided he loved Nora and told Diane that it was over and that he would not be joining her in her new life in Oregon. When her pleading failed to get results, on April 28th, Diane returned to Arizona to see Nick in person.

"I did not kiss her. I did not hug her I didn't tell her I loved her. I didn't say anything...I only said about twenty words to her the whole time she was there. I told her I wasn't going to Oregon. I told her I just didn't want to be a daddy. She talked at me - like always."[4]

Diane returned to Oregon alone.

The Shooting

It was exactly three weeks later that Diane Downs pulled up outside the McKenzie-Willamette Hospital with her children bleeding inside the car. 7-year-old Cheryl was already dead, and Christie, 8, and Danny, 3, were barely alive. Diane had a towel wrapped around her left arm, trying to stem the blood from the gunshot wound she had sustained almost exactly midway between her wrist and elbow.

As doctors tried frantically to save the lives of the two little ones, suspicion fell on the mother. On arrival at the hospital, the first person Diane called was her former lover, Nick, and not Steven, the children's father. Evidence started to mount against her, as her behavior belied that of a grieving mother in shock, and it became clearer that what they had was a case of filicide – Diane Downs had, in fact, murdered her own daughter and attempted to take the lives of her other two children.

That day, Diane had taken Christie, Cheryl and Danny to a friend's house in Marcola to see her horse. It was dark when they left, and Diane told the police that they had decided to go 'sightseeing' along the Old Mohawk Road, a deserted and dark stretch of road in the Springfield area. According to Diane, a bushy-haired stranger had flagged her down, and she had stopped to see if he needed help. Diane alleged that she had stepped out onto the road, and the man had demanded her car. When Diane refused, she said, the man leant into the car and shot her three children, before turning the gun on Diane and shooting her in her left arm. She maintained that she escaped by pretending to throw the car keys away, distracting the carjacker long enough to allow her the time to drive off at speed in order to get the heavily bleeding children to the hospital.

However, another motorist came forward and told police that he had driven behind Downs' car between the scene of the shooting and the hospital and that she had driven so slowly that the speed didn't even register on her speedometer. She was waiting for her children to bleed out, and die.

When the doctors broke the news to Diane that Cheryl hadn't survived, and that Christie and Danny were alive, although seriously ill, her reaction stunned them.

"Do you mean the bullet missed his heart? Gee whiz!"

Suspicion was further raised when Diane approached her daughter Christie's hospital bed, in intensive care. The child's reaction was one of terror – her eyes widened and her heart rate increased dramatically, from 104 bpm, to 147.

Police had one credible witness to the shooting – 8-year-old Christie Downs herself. At 3 years of age, little Danny was too young but Christie was old enough to be able to relay what she saw. The only problem was that Christie had suffered a stroke as a result of the shooting, and was unable to speak.

As pieces of the puzzle came together, detectives believed they had found the mother's motive for shooting her children. They travelled to Arizona to speak to her former lover, Nick. It was his statement which cemented the police's belief that Diane had committed the crime. He told police that he would never see Diane while the children were there.

*"I wouldn't be with her if the children were around," he explained. "It was an affair – it didn't seem right."*5

The police had their motive – Diane Downs wanted her children out of the way in the belief that her lover, Nick, would come back to her.

The Trial

On June 17th, 1974, Diane Downs was convicted of the murder of Cheryl Lynn Downs, and the attempted murder of Christie Anne Downs and Stephen Daniel Downs. Christie had recovered her speech and took the stand. It was the pivotal moment in the trial. When asked who had shot her siblings and herself, she stated tearfully that her mom had done it, and went on to describe the events.

In an effort to sway sympathy her way, Diane appeared at her trial heavily pregnant. She claimed it was because she missed her children, whom she was not allowed to see, so much.

During the trial, Diane Downs made allegations that she had been sexually abused by her father, Wes Frederickson, from the age of 11, and that her father had driven her out into the desert and ordered her to remove her blouse and bra. He vigorously denied these events, and Diane has since publicly retracted the allegations.

On sentencing, Judge Gregory Foote made it clear that he never wanted Downs to be freed, and sentenced her to life imprisonment, plus fifty years.

Ten days prior to sentencing, Diane gave birth to a little girl, who she named Amy. The baby was taken by the State and adopted shortly afterwards. Her name was changed to Rebecca Babcock.6

Downs was sent to the Oregon Women's Correctional Center in Salem, but in 1988 she escaped, by scaling an 18-foot high fence. Security was tightened around Christie and wheelchair-bound Danny, who had by this time been adopted by prosecutor Fred Hugi and his wife, Joanne, amid fears that Diane would come looking for her children. However, she was found 10 days later only four blocks from the prison in a house with four men. She had made no attempt to contact her children.

After her escape, and subsequent recapture, Diane Downs was sent to the maximum security Clinton Correctional Institution in New Jersey. In 1994 she was transferred to the California Department of Corrections and Rehabilitation, where she studied for, and was awarded, a degree in general studies. She was later incarcerated at the Valley State Prison for Women in Chowchilla, California, which is where she remains to date.

So far her requests for parole have been denied.

JANIE LOU GIBBS

Janie Lou Hickox was born on December 25th, Christmas day, 1932 in Cordele, Georgia. Cordele is now a town with just over 11 000 residents, and is proudly known as the Watermelon Capital of the World. The city is named after Cordelia Hawkins who was the eldest daughter of Colonel Samuel Hawkins, the president of the Savannah, Americus and Montgomery Railway. In November of 1864, the area temporarily served as the capital of Georgia, but Cordele as it is now knows was founded in 1888 as a junction between two major railroads: the Savannah, Americus and Montgomery line and the Georgia Southern and Florida. Notable people from the area include jazz and blues singers, sportsmen, a White House Press Secretary and the president of an international Christian TV network. Nobody suspected that a serial killer who would be a black widow was growing up in their midst.

There is not much information about Janie's upbringing, but it was strictly religious and she grew up in a fairly poor family. Janie was married to Charles Clayton Gibbs, a farmer, when she was only fifteen. The two moved to the nearby town of Arabi which was just under ten miles away from Cordele, a mere fifteen minutes by car. Both of these towns fall under the Crisp County district. Arabi now has a population of 586, with 185 hosueholds and 125 families living in the town. Janie and Charles were regular churchgoers, and they had three boys: Roger Ludean Gibbs, Melvin Watess Gibbs, and Marvin Ronald Gibbs. For eighteen years, they lived quiet and devoted lives on the farm until tragedy began to take blow after blow upon the family.

Janie was known for spending all of her spare time helping out at the church and for her day-care service that she ran in her home for children of working mothers. Accounts note that on most days Janie would have around twenty-five children at her house aside from her own sons. While some believed her to have almost fanatic religious beliefs, all members of Janie's church and community believed her to be sound of mind and to know the difference between right and wrong, testimonies that they would later make in the investigation. Nobody felt that Janie had any emotional or mental issues, and simply knew her as a devoted mother who held God and the church close to her heart. When she wasn't looking after children in the community, Janie was helping out with events around the church and other ways to support the congregation.

Just before the tragedies began to occur, Janie had travelled to Albany, Georgia for a doctor's appointment. There she had been diagnosed with Lou Gehrig's disease, a motor neurone disease that destroys muscle control, is also known as amyotrophic lateral sclerosis or ALS. The disease progresses from a stiffness of muscles to twitching while the person becomes increasingly weaker. Eventually, once their muscles have decreased in size enough, the patient has trouble with speaking, swallowing, and eventually breathing. Janie was very aware that her body would begin to systematically shut itself down. After her trial, her defense lawyer Frank Martin stated that this was one of the most tragic aspects of the case as far as he was concerned. Frank believed that due to Janie's acute awareness of how her illness would progress paired with her fanatic religious beliefs, she wanted everybody that was close to her in the world to go to heaven so that she would be with them when she finally passed. Although Janie never admitted this in court, the murder of her husband, three sons, and grandson, all of whom she loved dearly, suggests that this might have been a contributing factor to the decisions or delirium that ended in her intentionally poisoning five members of her family.

The first member of the family to go was her husband, Charles Clayton Gibbs, who died on the 21st January 1966 when he was only thirty-nine years old. Janie was an avid cook, and she always had home cooked meals ready for her family when they returned home from work or school. After having had one such meal, Charles collapsed in the family home and was taken to hospital. Janie went to the hospital to care for him and brought a flask of soup with her. After Charles was served this final meal, he died painfully from stomach cramps and convulsions. Years later, investigators realized that this soup must have been laced with a particularly strong dose of arsenic from rat poison that Janie had been giving him in trace amount in his meals and coffees.

When administered in small amounts like this, it can be very difficult to determine if somebody is a victim of arsenic poisoning unless a doctor thinks to specifically check for it. Arsenic poisoning can result in a host of different symptoms and organ failures, so it is often the case that medical professionals are waiting for more evidence to be able to provide a solid diagnosis while the victim continues to be poisoned by somebody close to them. Symptoms can include abdominal pain and cramping, diarrhea, vomiting, dark urine, dehydration, vertigo, delirium, shock, hair loss, and convulsions. Arsenic is flavorless and odorless, making it very difficult for somebody to connect their normal food and beverage consumption with their illness. Arsenic poisoning can affect the skin, liver, lungs, and kidneys, which is both why it is such a potentially fatal condition and why it is difficult to detect without a hunch. In the case of Charles, his death was written down to an undiagnosed liver disease that he had been suffering for some time. While the doctors wanted to perform an autopsy on her husband to be sure, Janie said that she didn't want him 'all cut up', and her wishes were respected.

The church community provided an overwhelming amount of support for the Gibbs family once Charles had passed. The entire congregation was shocked, Charles having seemed to be in such good health until recent times, and also because he was still so young. The Gibbs family were provided with company, meals, emotional support, and everything that the members of their church community could possibly extend. When the life insurance claim for Charles came through, Janie donated a significant portion of these funds to the church to demonstrate her thanks for everything that they had done and her belief in the community. Janie claimed that she and the boys would have to continue on as best they could, and that she felt that with the strength of the church community behind them they would be able to make it through. Even after their home burned down soon after Charles' death and the family moved back to Janie's home town of Cordele, Janie continued to offer day-care services for the children of working mothers. There has never been an investigation into the house burning down, but the timing is certainly curious. Is it possible that Janie felt this was the only way to justify moving her family back to her home town of Cordele? It is clear from the rest of her actions over this two year period that she wasn't thinking rationally, and perhaps she wanted to escape the physical environment where she had been married for all of those years. Whatever the reason, just as nobody suspected that Janie had anything to do with the death of her husband, there was no investigation into whether or not the house burned down due to arson.

It was around this time that the oldest Gibbs son Roger took notice of a girl in their congregation, Ellen Penny. A relationship began to blossom between them under the watchful eye of Janie. The two teenagers began to spend more and more time together at church events, and participated in the same activities together. If Roger was assigned the duty of retrieving the bibles at the end of a ceremony, Ellen would always be there too help him. Very soon the two began to date. Over the next year Roger and Ellen married and she became pregnant with their first child. Ellen began living at the Gibb's residence, but this relationship and pregnancy was against a dark backdrop. It is difficult to say whether Janie took an immediate dislike to Ellen, or whether she did not want her son getting married and having a child so early like she had herself. Perhaps she wanted a different life for him, or harbored some resentment on being married off at such a young age. Either way,

Janie never had a good relationship with Ellen and many times would behave as if she almost didn't register her existence.

Only months after Charles' death, Marvin began to develop the same symptoms as his father had. Having moved house and town, perhaps the rest of the family felt a separation with losing their father and like this wouldn't happen again with their youngest brother. There are no records of comments from the brothers or the community being concerned that Marvin would go the same way as his father, but sure enough, nine months after his father had died, Marvin Ronald Gibbs died on the 29th August 1966. Marvin too was determined to have an undiagnosed liver disease just like his father had, and Janie once again refused to have an autopsy performed. Perhaps Janie felt that performing an autopsy was an ungodly act that would in some way affect the chances of her family members getting into heaven? While the largest reason was most certainly to protect her own interests and for her to be able to complete her task, autopsy is a process rejected by many faiths and traditions. The police and staff at the insurance company pushed for autopsies as they felt that two deaths of this nature so close together and in one family didn't make sense. At this time, some members of the church community began to have suspicions about the deaths in the Gibbs family, but nobody wanted to be the one to come forward and accuse the pious and highly involved church member that Janie was. For many, there was still a huge disconnect. So even though the insurance company and the police of Crisp County were pressing for an autopsy on the body of young Marvin, Janie still had the support of the community enough to request that this procedure not be undertaken. Despite their suspicions, many in the community still felt that Janie wouldn't be capable of doing such a thing, particularly when it was to her own family that she seemed to have such an active devotion to.

Once again the church community poured support for the Gibb's family, offering counsel and companionship for Janie and her two remaining boys. When Marvin's life insurance came through, Janie once again provided a large portion of this claim to the church, which was undergoing significant renovations. While some began to talk about Janie seeming to almost be enjoying her new lifestyle, never being seen in the same dress and buying a new car, they could not help notice how generous she was also being with these funds. Those members of the community who still had faith in Janie chalked this spending down to a way to cope with her losses. However, Ellen Penny remained highly suspicious of Janie Gibbs. She didn't know how to speak out about her, both because she needed to live with the family and because she was so young, but after Marvin's death Ellen was certain that what was happening to the Gibbs family was no random or hereditary tragedy. Then, Melvin also began to fall ill.

As Melvin (often referred to in some articles as Lester) began to follow the path of his father and younger brother, the sixteen year old started to experience dizzy spells. Some people in the community attributed these headaches to puberty as the boy was sixteen. By this point, with such serious difficulties in the family, it is a wonder that Melvin's complaints weren't taken more seriously. He went downhill sharply. The doctors, not wanting to claim his death as another bout of undiagnosed liver disease that they weren't certain of, labeled his death a result of hepatitis. Once again a claim was made for life insurance, a portion donated to the church, and support lavished upon the Gibbs' family. At this point, Ellen became terrified for the life of her husband, herself, and their unborn child.

About a month after Melvin's death, Ellen and Roger's baby, Raymond, was born. Everybody noticed that Janie's mood lifted, and the community felt that this is where the horror ended for the Gibb's family. Janie was thrilled with her grandson, even though she had been so early married herself and her son had had his first child so early, making Janie a grandmother at thirty-four. Janie often used to show the baby to anybody who came around to the house, and would often be seen out with Raymond around the city. Ellen began to feel at ease around this time as Janie seemed to have changed entirely. The way that she interacted with Ellen seemed to have improved, and it seemed that the way that Janie went about all of her daily tasks with a different air.

However, even the baby began to fall ill soon. Ellen was in a state of desperation and didn't know what to do, the child only being one month old. The young girl has nobody that she could turn to, and didn't feel confident enough to make an accusation against Janie, even to her own husband. Despite the fact that Raymond was perfectly healthy, he died of an apparent heart condition. Everybody who was close to the Gibbs were completely shocked to hear of Raymond's death, and this is the point that many members of the congregation became highly suspicious of Janie. However, nobody did anything to prevent her from claiming the fifth and final member of her immediate family, her eldest and grieving son, with both Roger and Ellen still living with her at the time.

In the weeks after their baby died, Roger began to fall ill. Ellen, who was still under twenty at this age, had still not found the courage or the means to speak out against Janie. This may have been due to her living situation, or perhaps due to the sudden death of her son, but as Roger grew increasingly ill Ellen could do nothing but watch him deteriorate. She notes that during this time her husband constantly had red eyes, had visible rings around these, and was always pale and lacking in energy. He also used to get very severe headaches, but wasn't the type of person that liked to talk about any suffering that he was experiencing. The most that he would discuss these headaches was when he would be in such pain that he would be flinching. Ellen would ask if his head was giving him trouble again, to which he would respond with short and basic answers. Roger eventually found himself bedridden, being cared for by his mother. Despite what had happened to his father, two brothers, and own son, Roger never shared any suspicions about his mother with Ellen. It is entirely possible that he had figured out what was going on, being the last left, but didn't know how to get himself out of the situation.

Over the weeks, Roger's health got worse and worse. Ellen remembers overhearing an argument between Roger and his mother where he was repeatedly saying

"You did it! You did this to me!"

He was saying it over and over again as fiercely as he was able to in his deteriorated state. Ellen did not fully understand the conversation as she made sure that she kept out of sight. She asked Roger about it later in private, but he didn't reveal anything further and simply said that he and his mother had been squabbling over something. Ellen began to wonder whether she was paranoid about the situation, but it seemed that everything was pointing towards Janie's involvement in not only Roger's sickness but the suspicious deaths of the other four. Ellen stayed by her husband and cared for him as best she could, watching on as Janie nursed her son.

When Roger was eventually placed in hospital, Janie and Ellen spent nearly all of their time there. After a couple of days, Ellen noticed that Janie was in the habit of taking the water jug that the hospital placed in their room, tipping it down the sink, and replacing it with her own water. When Ellen asked her why she was doing this, Janie claimed that the hospital water had too much sulfur and that it hurt his throat. It was later realized that she was feeding her last remaining immediate family member increasing doses of arsenic through the water. Janie forced Roger to drink the water in large gulps and often. Once again, it is difficult to understand why this behavior was accepted by nurses, and also why nobody gave Roger testing for arsenic poisoning when four members of his family had died so suspiciously. However, even though this was a fairly common way for women to kill at the time, it is not until later years that we realized the signs and hints that might have saved the Gibbs family from their wife and mother.

One day, Janie asked Ellen to give Roger some water. Janie filled up a tall glass and placed it in Ellen's hand. Ellen gave Roger a small sip, but Janie demanded that he finish the whole glass, telling her that his throat is dry and he needs more. Ellen tipped the whole glass of water down her husband's throat, unknowingly giving him the final and strongest dose of arsenic. Perhaps Janie had been hoping that the blame might be placed on Ellen, or maybe she got satisfaction out of Ellen being the one that finally killed Roger, Janie having never been too keen on the girl. As Janie didn't want an autopsy on Roger, just like it was for the others, it is hard to say whether this act was a final insurance in her mind of her not being guilty of the crime, or whether it was the latter and she got satisfaction out of Ellen killing her spouse unintentionally. It is also possible, with Roger being left for last, that she was the least willing to kill him and needed Ellen to perform this final duty. After all, it would have made sense to kill the older two sons first and leave the younger one in her care, Marvin being so young and the least able of all three brothers to be able to take any action against his mother even if he had figured out what was happening. This suggests that Roger might have been somewhat of a favorite of Janie's, and that she wanted as much time with him as she could. Whatever the reason, Roger died soon after receiving the dose. He was only nineteen, and this finished Janie's work, whether it was insurance fraud or what she perceived to be God's work.

Just as she had with her two younger sons and her husband, Janie attempted to stop medical professionals from undertaking autopsies on Roger and Raymond Gibbs. However, as Ellen was the wife and mother, she has the rights of next of kin. Autopsies were performed that revealed extremely high levels of arsenic in Roger's organs, around twenty times that which you would expect to find in a body during an autopsy where arsenic has not been the cause of death. It was at this time that the Crisp County police called for the bodies of Charles, Marvin, and Melvin to be exhumed. People crowded around at the graveyard to watch while the bodies were taken out of the ground and placed on blue tarps. People began to say that they had thought there was something suspicious the whole time. A lot of guilt began to spread through the community. What if they had mentioned something earlier? Would they have at least been able to save the lives of Roger and his infant son? Mothers who had given their children to Janie to look after day in and day out felt embarrassed about their judgment of her character. This time the sympathy poured out for young Ellen who has lost her home, husband, and baby all within the space of a month. All five murders were committed in a short period of time, between 1966 and 1967. In all, Janie had received $31 000 in life insurance payments and given around ten percent of this to the church, but now she would have to answer for the crimes that she had done against those in the world that trusted her the most. Eric Hickey who has performed a study on female serial killers including Janie Lou Gibbs in 1991 claims that "These are the *quiet killers*, every bit as lethal as male serial murderers, but we are seldom aware of one in our midst because of their low visibility." Hickey also found that it takes an average of eight years to catch a female serial killer, nearly double what it takes on average to identify and arrest male serial killers.

Janie was arrested on Christmas Eve 1967, the day before her thirty-fifth birthday. She admitted to having killed all five of her immediate family members, but claimed that she didn't have a motive for doing so. While many people claim that she did this for the insurance money, there is still the chance that she genuinely committed the crimes in the name of her fanatic religious beliefs, wanting her family to be with her in heaven.

By February, Janie was determined to be insane and not fit for a trial but it was still agreed that she should not be able to live out her life in the community as she had been before. Janie took up residence at a state mental hospital where she served as a hospital cook, living there until 1976. At this time, multiple people had testified that they thought Janie was aware enough of her actions that she should have to deal with their legal ramifications. On May 9th 1976, Janie was convicted for her crimes and handed down five life sentences, one for each family member that she had poisoned. Janie's sister came to visit her in an attempt to understand the things that Janie has done, but found that she was largely nonresponsive and bewildered. The first question that her sister asked was *Why did you kill your family, Janie?* To which Janie responded she didn't know. Her sister attempted again, saying *Do you feel guilty?* Janice once again responded that she didn't know, seeming to be removed and numbed to the situation. Her sister made one final attempt to reach out to Janie and understand what had happened, asking *Can I do anything to help you?* For the third time, Janie responded that she didn't know. Her sister continued to visit her in jail in an attempt to understand more about Janie, what she had done, and what she was going through. But it seemed that no matter how much she tried, Janie was like a shell of what she had previously been.

She came up for parole seventeen times but was denied on each occasion. In April of 1999, due to her failing health as a result of Parkinson's disease, Janie was released into her sister's care. The last years of her life were spent in a wheel chair at a nursing home in Douglasville, Georgia, where she died on February 7th 2010. She now rests in the Sunrise Memorial Gardens at Lithia Springs in Douglas County, Georgia

HUSBAND KILLER : THE TRUE STORY OF AUDREY MARIE HILLEY

26

ANNA DELANEY

Audrey Marie Hilley

"That woman was pitiful," said Janice Hinds, 50, one of two neighbours who called police and cared for Hilley after spotting her sprawled on the deck of Thomason's home.

"We didn't know she was Marie Hilley. She didn't look like Marie Hilley," said Hinds, who grew up in the same Blue Mountain cotton-mill town as Hilley. "Marie Hilley was a sophisticated lady. She had pride in her looks, her dress."[1]

Her Early Life

Audrey Marie Hilley was born on June 4th, 1933 in Blue Mountain, Alabama. Her parents, Huey and Lucille Frazier, worked hard at the Linen Mill to provide for their family, and Marie (as she was known) was often looked after by relatives when her mother returned to work shortly after she was born.

Huey and Lucille loved their only child but showed their love with material things rather than affection and time. She was always well-dressed and had nice things, and as a result, Marie became rather spoilt. She was well known for her temper tantrums when things didn't go her way, and her parents, possibly out of guilt for not being there, rarely checked her for her behaviour.[2]

The Fraziers were proud people and were determined that their only child would not spend her life working in the same mills as they, and most of the town's inhabitants, had always done. They wanted more for their daughter and instilled in her an ambition to be a secretary, a lofty ambition for someone from a mill town.

In 1945, the Fraziers moved from Blue Mountain to Anniston, and Marie enrolled at Quintard Junior High School. Anniston was a whole new world to the girl who had felt she was above the rest in her old hometown. Marie went from being a big fish in a small pond to a small fish in a much more upscale lake, and for the first time in her life found herself at a disadvantage. In Anniston, all the girls wore nice dresses and what was more, some of their parents were the owners of the same mills that Marie's parents worked at.

Marie threw herself into her studies, making a name for herself as a diligent, intelligent student, and she integrated herself into new social circles – her friends were from privileged families and Marie wanted to be a part of that.

It wasn't just the teachers for whom Marie stood out, though. She was also a pretty girl and had her fair share of the attention from the boys, too. In fact, by the end of the 7th grade of Junior High School, Marie Hilley had been voted the prettiest girl in school by the yearbook staff.

It was around this time that 16-year-old Frank Hilley noticed 12-year-old Marie, and by the time he graduated High School, he was in love.[3]

Frank and Marie

In contrast to the Frazier family, who loved their daughter but showed no affection, Frank Hilley's family was warm and affectionate. The Hilleys worked in the other big industry of the area – pipe making - and even though they did not have much money, Clarence and Carrie Hilley made a happy, comfortable home for their three children – Frank, Jewel and Freeda.

Marie's parents did not approve of Frank – he was not from one of the affluent families of Anniston and Huey and Lucille wanted more for their daughter – but Marie was happy to be Frank's girl, and in return, he treated her like a princess.

Frank joined the Navy after finishing High School and was assigned to Guam but the distance between them bothered Frank. He was worried that with him so far away, and with so much time apart, Marie might find someone else so, on May 8th, 1951, before 17-year-old Marie had even finished High School, the young couple married.

Married Life

Marie remained in Anniston to finish her education and then joined Frank in Long Beach, California before the couple moved to Boston where Frank finished his stint in the Navy. It was while they were in Boston that they discovered Marie was pregnant with their first child, and the couple moved back to Anniston and bought a small home. Frank secured a job with a local foundry, and Marie found work as a secretary. Like all couples, the pair had their ups and downs, but for the most part, they seemed happy.

Their first child, Michael Hilley, was born on November 11th, 1952.

The Troubles Begin

Marie had been brought up to want the best of everything. While Frank was still in the Navy he had sent all of his paychecks home to his young wife, and yet when the time had come for her to join her new husband in California she had no money to pay for the journey. She had been spending his wages without telling him, and his parents had had to finance Marie's travel in order for her to join her new husband.

Despite the extra financial burdens having a young baby places on a family, Marie's spending didn't decrease. She wanted nice clothes and expensive home furnishings, and Frank, not liking to upset his wife, gave in to her, just as her parents had when she was a girl. Marie was a woman who was used to getting her own way.[4]

In 1959 Marie's behaviour began to become more sinister. She started taunting Frank, waving love letters she said were from other men in front of him but not letting him read them. She would then leave the torn up pieces where her husband could find them. Frank pieced them together, and it became clear that his wife had written them herself. When he confronted her she said she was afraid he didn't love her anymore and wanted to make him jealous.

By this time, Marie was spending double her take-home pay from her own job on fine clothes and luxuries. To prevent Frank, who was extremely responsible financially, from finding out she would get up early in the morning to check the mail and hide the bills.

Marie became pregnant again, and on January 14th, 1960 she gave birth to a baby daughter, whom they named Carol Marie.[5]

Carol

By the time Carol was born, things should have been looking up for the family. Frank had been promoted at work, and Marie had developed a reputation as a first class executive secretary. However, as the family's income rose, so did Marie's spending. Furthermore, she was becoming known for a peculiar situation at work. While her bosses loved her for her politeness and diligence, her co-workers greatly disliked her. They found her to be very judgemental of those around her and felt that she put on airs and graces and acted as if her co-workers were 'beneath' her. When she became disliked she would leave, and complain to friends and family that her colleagues had 'ganged up' on her and driven her from her job. Her employers, though, always gave her exemplary references, and she never found it difficult to get another job. In fact, Marie Hilley worked for some of the most powerful and affluent men in Anniston.[6]

Marie was disappointed with her daughter, Carol. She wanted her daughter to wear pretty dresses and have bows in her hair, while Carol was more of a tomboy and would often go to football games with her father. The pair developed a close father/daughter relationship and Marie was deeply resentful and jealous. She lamented the fact that her daughter was not feminine and demure and the pair argued constantly. Marie was much closer to her son, Mike, and like her parents before her never dished out discipline. Materially, the children wanted for nothing. Emotionally, it was a different story.

Going Up in the World

In 1962, Marie instigated a move to McClellan Boulevard, which was much closer to the houses of the affluent residents of Anniston that she so desperately tried to emulate. She felt that they were 'her' people. That same year, Marie's parents – Huey and Lucille moved in with the Hilleys.[7]

Marie's behaviour was becoming more and more out of control, and Frank was becoming increasingly concerned. He would often sit up with her during the night as she shook violently, unable to calm her. Perhaps the financial hole she had dug for the family was beginning to take its toll on Marie's psyche – by this time she had opened a Post Office Box and was having some of her bills sent there in order to avoid detection by Frank.

When the money ran out Marie started taking out loans. Frank was a well-respected man in the area and loans were secured against his good name and standing in the community. But creditors became concerned when bills and loan payment dates came and went without being settled, as Frank had always been a man who paid on time.[8]

On December 11th, 1965, Marie's father, Huey, died of cancer at the age of 57.[9]

In 1972, Mike graduated from High School and decided to pursue a career in the ministry, for which he went away to college.

Marie's behaviour towards her daughter, Carol, became more extreme. She often accused her of being a lesbian and would rant at Carol's female friends. Her paranoia at being found out in the lies regarding money must have been affecting her, because she also, around this time, stopped Frank from talking to his friends on the 'phone. It was also around this period of time that Frank Hilley became sick.[10]

Frank

During 1974 Frank had long periods of sickness. He put his frequent illnesses down to something he'd eaten, but soon the fatigue, vomiting and nausea could not be explained away by food. One day Frank came home from work early after succumbing to yet another bout of sickness, to find his wife in bed with her boss. His wife's spending suddenly made sense – she was sleeping with her employers for money. Frank was disgusted with his wife's behaviour but felt too ill and weak to deal with it. Instead, he turned to his son, Mike, who was by this time an ordained minister.[11]

However, that phone call, in which Frank arranged to meet Mike in Georgia where he now lived, was overheard by Audrey, who was listening in on an extension. From that moment on, Frank's symptoms worsened considerably, and he became seriously ill.[12]

On May 19th, 1975 Frank couldn't stand it any longer, and he consulted Dr Earl Jones, who diagnosed him initially with a viral stomach ache.[13] Dr Earl prescribed various medications, but nothing seemed to be helping. Frank's sister Freeda came to visit him, and he told her that he feared he was going to die, as he had never been so sick. He also told her that Marie had been administering him medicine via a syringe on the Dr's orders.[14]

On May 23rd, 1975, Frank was admitted to the Regional Medical Center. Tests indicated liver failure, and subsequently infectious hepatitis.[15] Frank was desperately ill, jaundiced and hallucinating. Mike, who had travelled to be with his father, had to restrain Frank from jumping out of the window. In the early hours of May 25th, Mike left the hospital to pick up his Grandmothers so that they could see Frank, but when he returned his mother was asleep and his father was dead. Frank Hilley was 45.[16]

Because of Frank's sudden death, an autopsy was performed, with Marie's blessing. Tests showed that Frank did indeed have hepatitis, along with swelling of the lungs and kidneys, inflammation of the stomach, and bilateral pneumonia.[17]

Life After Frank

With Frank's death being confirmed as being of natural causes, Marie made a claim on his life insurance and received a payment of

$31,140.[18] Marie went on a spending spree, indulging her love of luxury items. She bought new clothes, jewelery, and a new car. Her mother, Lucille, was still living with Marie and Carol and received a diamond ring. Carol herself was treated to numerous gifts, including a car and a stereo. It was hardly the behaviour of a grieving widow.[19]

In 1976 Mike and his then wife Teri moved in with the family. Shortly after Frank's death, Lucille had been diagnosed with cancer. Her health was failing and they were happy to help. However, it wasn't a good move for the young couple. Marie was restless, and often complained to anyone who would listen that nobody loved her, and would frequently complain about her boss and her job. She was highly dissatisfied with her life, and to make matters worse Marie and Carol fought endlessly, making family life fraught. Mike would often find himself torn between his mother, who would constantly demand his attention, and his wife, Teri, who had begun experiencing ill health since moving in with Marie. Hospitalised four times with illness, Teri also suffered a miscarriage, and the young couple decided to move out.

They found an apartment and were ready to move in, but the night before their move Marie's house caught fire. Mike and Teri moved into their apartment, with Marie, Carol and Lucille in tow. Repairs were soon made to Marie's house, but the night before his mother was due to go home, Mike's neighbour's apartment suffered the same fate and went up in flames. Mike and Teri had no choice but to move back in with Marie, Carol and Lucille. They were back where they began.[20]

A Strange Series of Events
Mike and Teri finally found their own home and moved away from Marie. On January 4th, 1977, Lucille lost her battle against widespread, aggressive cancer. Marie again came into money – a small sum of $600 from a burial policy.

Marie became well known to the local police. She was constantly reporting strange occurrences at her home. As well as petty thefts, she claimed that a fire had been started in her closet late one night. Coincidentally, Marie's neighbour, Doris Ford reported an almost identical fire in her own house (to which Marie had a key) the same night. There followed a succession of reports by both women of nuisance phone calls and other grievances.

Marie came up with many theories about where the harassment of both herself and her neighbour was coming from. She told Detective Gary Caroll that she suspected someone at the phone company of making the calls, as the calls seemed only to happen when the trace was taken off of her phone. She also claimed that one of her former employers had tried to force her to have sex and was harassing her because of her refusal. Yet another theory put forward by Marie was that, shortly after Frank's death, two men had arrived at her house demanding repayment of gambling debts.

When police put a trace on Doris Ford's phone, however, the calls were traced back to the Jenkins Manufacturing Plant, which just so happened to be where Marie was working.[21]

In 1978, Marie and Carol moved to Florida to live with Mike and Teri. Carol had just graduated, and Marie found herself a job in an office. Her out of control spending habits continued to cause problems when she ran up over $600 on Mike's credit card, promising to pay him back. This living arrangement only lasted a few short months, however, before Marie and Carol returned to Anniston.[22]

Mike and Teri were happy to see Marie leave. By that time they had a baby son called Joshua, and Mike feared that Marie would take the baby and disappear as she seemed to have an unhealthy fixation on him.[23]

Carol's Turn

Marie had no home of her own to return to when she and Carol moved back to Anniston. At first, they stayed with Freeda, Frank's sister, and then they moved in with Carrie Hilley, Frank's mother.

Once they were settled at Carrie's house, the strange happenings recommenced. Items went missing, phone lines were cut, and small fires were started. Illness also struck the household – Carrie Hilley started suffering from nausea and vomiting.

Marie started a new job, and very quickly started an affair with her boss, Harold Dillard, and began manipulating him to leave his wife. At the same time, she also started seeing Calvin Robertson, an old school friend. Calvin believed Marie when she told him she had cancer and needed expensive treatment, and he gladly gave her the money for the 'fictitious' illness. When Marie told him some time later that she was now cancer-free he was elated, and so smitten that he would have done anything for her.

It was also during this time that Marie began buying insurance policies. Not only did she take out fire insurance, cancer insurance, and her own life insurance, she also took out insurance policies on the lives of her two children. Mike was insured for $25,000 while Carol had two policies on her life, totalling $39,000.

Carol's senior prom came in April 1979. During the evening Carol started to feel ill. It wasn't enough to make her leave the party, though, so she ignored her symptoms. The next day, however, she was so ill during a church service that she had to leave the service early and vomited in the car park. Coincidentally, Carrie Hilley had also taken ill at church and was taken to hospital after fainting.[24]

By August 1979 Carol had been admitted to the Emergency Room several times with nausea and vomiting. After yet another episode of sickness in August, Marie gave her daughter an injection into her hip, which she said would ease the nausea. Instead of easing, however, Carol's illness took a serious downturn. Not only did the injection not ease Carol's sickness, it also caused her fingers and legs to become numb and weak.

On August 22nd, 1979 she was admitted to the Anniston Hospital by Dr Warren Sarrell. When, by August 29th Dr Sarrell had been unable to find a cause for Carol's symptoms, he sent her for a psychiatric evaluation at the Carraway Methodist Hospital in Birmingham. While under the care of Dr John Elmore, Carol was given two further injections by her mother – injections which, she was told, would help with her weak legs. She told Carol that the injections had been supplied by Doris Ford, who was a registered nurse, and that Carol could tell no-one as Doris would get into trouble if she was found out.

On September 18th, 1979, with Carol still in the hospital, Marie asked Dr Elmore what was wrong with her daughter. He told her that she was suffering from vitamin deficiencies and malnutrition, and, in his opinion, lead poisoning. Carol took exception to this diagnosis and, against Dr Elmore's advice, discharged Carol from the hospital.

On September 19th, Carol was once again admitted to the hospital, this time to the University of Alabama Hospital in Birmingham. The same day, Marie was arrested as her fraudulent ways finally caught up with her. Her arrest was what, ultimately, saved Carol's life. Marie was taken in for questioning, and Carol was examined by Dr Brian Thompson, who noticed that, along with the numbness in her hands and feet, Carol also had striations on her nails, called Aldridge Mee's Lines. He explained that these markings were typical of arsenic poisoning, and ordered tests on Carol's hair.

The initial findings revealed that Carol had over 50 times the normal arsenic level of human hair. Shockingly, when more detailed tests were carried out on October 3rd, 1979 they showed that the hair close to Carol's scalp had over 100 times the normal levels, while hair further down the hair shaft the levels were lower, right down to zero at the ends. This indicated, according to Forensic Scientist John Case, that Carol had been systematically poisoned with arsenic over a period of four to eight months, with the dosages given in increasingly higher strengths.

Furthermore, with Marie unable to be with her daughter, Carol's conditioned improved dramatically during her time at the hospital.[25]

On the strength of these findings, Frank Hilley's body was exhumed, and once again large levels of arsenic were found. His cause of death was changed to that of arsenic poisoning. The same substance was also discovered to have been present in both Lucille Frazier and Carrie Hilley (who had died recently) at the time of their deaths, although not fatal amounts.[26]

On October 9th, 1979, while still incarcerated for the fraudulent charges, Marie Hilley was arrested for the attempted murder of Carol. As part of their ongoing, and increasingly serious, investigations the Anniston police found a vial in Marie's purse – a vial which testing confirmed contained arsenic.

On November 9th, 1979, Marie made bail and was released, under the name of Emily Stephens, to a local motel. However, Marie was not going to just sit and await her trial, and somewhere between October 9th and October 18th, Marie disappeared. A note was found in her motel room, suggesting that she 'might' have been kidnapped.

Audrey Marie Hilley was now a fugitive and would remain so for more than three years.[27]

A New Identity

There were only a few clues for the police to go on after Marie disappeared. Margaret Key, Marie's Aunt, reported that her home had been broken into and that her car and some clothes had disappeared. The police called in the FBI, but once the car was found abandoned in Georgia the trail went cold very quickly.

On January 11th, 1980, Marie Hilley, still a fugitive, was indicted for the murder of her husband, Frank Hilley.

Marie, meanwhile, had assumed a new identity in Florida. Robbi Hannon, as she was now known, was working her charm on a man called John Homan. Robbi told John tales of her imaginary tragic past, and John, who hadn't had the easiest of lives himself, fell for both the stories and for Robbi. She told him that she had lost her children in a car accident and John felt as though he had found a kindred spirit.

He fell in love, hook, line, and sinker.

On May 29th, 1981 Robbi and John were married, after which they moved to Marlow, New Hampshire. They both found work there and rented a house. Robbi's new job was in customer service at the Central Screw Corporation, where she excelled. The men found her to be fun, while her co-workers, for the most part, found her pleasant, although a few took a dislike to her. She regaled the staff with stories of a wealthy family in Texas, whose fortune she would inherit one day, and garnered sympathy by telling them about her two children dying in a car accident.

She would also talk of an identical twin sister called Teri Martin, who lived in Texas, making frequent reference to her.

Robbi would, from time to time, complain of searing headaches, and told John that she was seeking treatment from specialists. Until one day, Robbi came to John and told him it had been discovered that she was suffering from an incurable blood disease. It was her twin sister, Teri, who would be looking after Robbi when she made one last trip to Texas in search of a cure, and in September 1982, Robbi left Marlow to seek treatment.

Of course, there was no incurable disease, and no twin sister, either. Robbi only stayed in Texas for a few days, and then made her way to Florida, where she bleached her hair blond, and found work as a secretary, using the name Teri Martin. During her six weeks at her new job, Teri confided in her boss, Jack McKenzie, about her terminally ill twin sister Robbie. In early November, Teri called Jack and told him Robbi had died, and that she was needed in New Hampshire.

On November 10th, 'Teri' called John Homan and told him his wife had died, and the following day she flew back to New Hampshire.

During her time away, 'Teri' had lost a lot of weight, and changed her hair color to blond, so John easily accepted that this was his dead wife's twin sister. The pair went to the local paper and placed an obituary for Robbi, and then John took Teri to his wife's workplace – The Central Screw Corporation – and introduced the workers to Robbi's twin sister. While some of the staff accepted Teri's appearance, some did not and were highly suspicious.

Teri insisted on moving in with John Homan, saying they needed to help each other grieve, and she found herself a job as a secretary at a book printing company.

Meanwhile, the suspicions were still rising at Robbi's old workplace, and a few of the doubters decided to take a closer look into Robbi's obituary. Their suspicions were confirmed when they discovered that the details mentioned in the paper were fictitious, and they took those suspicions to the police.

Arrested

On January 12th, 1983, the police apprehended Teri at work. They had been watching her and thought she might be another fugitive, Terry Lynn Clifton. However, when they asked her her name she told them it was Audrey Marie Hilley, and that she was wanted for fraud. The local police ran a check on her name and discovered that she was wanted for much more than bad checks.

On January 19th, 1983, Marie was brought back to Anniston. Carol was desperate to see her mother, to find some answers, but although Marie professed her love for her daughter she gave no explanation for the poisoning. Prosecutors were worried that Carol's love for her mother would go in Marie's favour and that Carol would not say anything against her mother.

They needn't have worried.

Carol's testimony about her mother giving her the injections was solid. Marie had told her attorneys that after her arrest in 1979 she had been interviewed but she failed to mention that that interview had been recorded. During that interview, Marie admitted to giving Carol the injections and the recording was there for all to hear. Carol's defense fell apart.

The jury needed only three hours to return their verdicts – guilty of the murder of Frank Hilley, and of the attempted murder of Carol Hilley.

Judge Sam Monk sentenced Marie to life imprisonment for Frank's murder, plus twenty years for the poisonings, and on June 9th, 1983, Marie was taken to Tutwiler State Women's Prison in Wetumpka, Alabama.

Marie's Escape

Marie was a perfect prisoner. She never caused trouble and was classified as a minimum security prisoner. This classification meant that she was eligible for leave from the prison. Between late 1986 and February 1987, Marie had left prison for eight hours on four occasions, returning on time with each leave.

On February 19th, 1987, Marie left the prison on a three-day leave pass. John had, by this time, moved to Anniston so that he and his wife could spend her leave together whenever they could.

On February 22nd, Marie arranged to meet John at her parents' graves. Marie never showed up, and John found, instead, a note from his wife.

"I hope you will be able to forgive me," it read. *"I'm getting ready to leave. It will be best for everybody. We'll be together again. Please give me an hour to get out of town."*

John took the note to the police, and, given Marie's past cunning, they assumed she was already far out of state, and started, once again, searching for her.[28]

Her Death

Marie hadn't gone far. On February 26th, 1987, Aniston police received a phone call. Marie had been found huddled behind a house, apparently having wandered in the woods for four days. The weather had been terrible – heavy rain and low temperatures – and Marie was suffering from hypothermia and delirium. Marie started having convulsions, and, in the ambulance on the way to the hospital, Audrey Marie Hilley took her last breath.

On February 28th, 1987, Marie was buried next to her husband, Frank, at their children's request.[29] Her second husband, John Homan, died two years later in 1989 while working as a caretaker in Anniston. He intervened in a fight and was stabbed to death. Marie's note to John, in which she said that they would be together again, had come true a lot sooner than anyone would have predicted.[30]

HUSBAND KILLER TRACEY GRISSOM

42

Claiming to be a victim of rape and other abuses, a distraught Tracey Grissom would travel to her ex-husband Hunter's workplace and shoot him six times in the back, receiving a twenty-five-year life sentence for his murder.

Her defense attorney would argue that Tracey was motivated by post-traumatic stress disorder caused by her Hunter's constant abuse and sexual assaults. One jury member had even asked the judge to be lenient in her sentencing as they were not allowed to hear details of her Hunter's alleged abuses (beatings, rape, sodomy).

But what really happened in the years that led up to May 15th, 2012? Was she in fact the victim of years of abuse by a psychotic husband? Or did she want to cash in on his $100,000 life insurance policy?

INSTANT ATTRACTION

The couple would meet during a dinner party in 2003 in Tuscaloosa, Alabama. Tracey was twenty-one years old and going through a divorce. She had a son, James Michael, from the previous marriage.

Family and friends would describe the union as "love at first sight." Hunter was blown away by the young Tracey's blue eyes and facial beauty.

"For him, it was love at first sight," crime author William Phelps said. "She was gorgeous."

A whirlwind courtship would ensue and the couple would elope in 2004.

"In the beginning, it was good," Tracey told CBS' 48 hours. "We had a friendship. Just your normal, honeymoon phase marriage."

"He was fun," Tracey said. "And he was attractive."

Hunter was two years younger than Tracey, however, and his mother felt that he had jumped the gun too early in the relationship.

Her words proved to be prophetic as after only eight months into the marriage, the marriage went south.

According to Tracey, their marital problems began with Hunter's drug addiction.

"I had caught him smoking marijuana," Tracey said. "Doing illegal things could cause a problem and I couldn't risk losing my son over."

Tracey claimed that she threatened her new spouse with a divorce but Hunter gave her his word that he would stop with his drug use. She stated that the relationship improved and the decided to start a construction company together.

"I took out an equity line to start a company," Tracey said. "Which was Grissom Construction. It was all in my name."

Hunter specialized in building elaborate boat docks. He had an artistic eye and could do docks, stairs, and other accouterments. The business began to grow in short order.

"They're going to take on the world," Phelps said. "They're going to be entrepreneurs and they're gonna make it."

They then had a daughter of their own, Anna Grace. The child was a long time coming for the couple. They had been trying for a long time as Tracey had five miscarriages before Anna Grace was born.

"She was premature," Tracey recalled. "Her heart and lungs were not developed. A very stressful time."

Behind closed doors things were rocky. On the surface, however, things looked good. They had a young family and were making money.

"All-American family," Phelps said. "White-picket fence. The whole nine yards. Middle-class. Suburbia. Maybe the Prince Charming that she's been waiting for."

But again, this was only on the surface. Tracey harbored secrets of her own. One of which was her own addiction to prescription drugs.

"Psychologically, there's something going on here," Phelps said. "There's something going on behind those beautiful eyes and it ain't good."

Tracey would often turn on on the children, showing off her temper. Then she would turn on Hunter.

"This would cause friction in the marriage," Phelps said. "And where there's friction, there's fire."

SETTING THE STAGE

Tracey would later state that Hunter would "act strangely" shortly before she filed divorce. She was a registered nurse and gave him an over-the-counter drug test. According to her, Hunter tested posted for marijuana, Oxycontin, opiates, and methamphetamine.

Hunter would later be arrested for marijuana possession but his family would insist that he never did the harder drugs.

Tracey would file for divorce in the summer of 2010 after six years of marriage. According to her, this would prompt physical abuse from Hunter.

Hunter had to move out but their divorce agreement would allow him access to the home.

"In September of 2010," Tracey recalled. "That was the first time he physically hit me. It (the abuse) got progressively worse. He had made the comments that if I told anybody he would kill me. I believed him."

Hunter' co-workers and family members would have a different take on the situation, however. His co-workers remembered a time when she tracked him down at one of the jobs and made a scene.

"She's screaming, jumping on him," Hunter's co-worker said. "Said something about him having another girlfriend and used the expression about, 'You are mine. I'll kill you. I'll kill you. You are mine."

"She's borderline demonic," Hunter's mother said. " mean, I absolutely believe—that she is that troubled."

Hunter's family continued to believe that he did not abuse Tracey.

"He did not have an abusive, an angry bone in his body," Hunter's aunt Gina said. "In fact, we kind of laughed at him because he was too laid-back."

The divorce was finalized in October of 2010.

EVIDENCE OF ABUSE?

Loran Richards was the first of Tracey's friends to notice the minor injuries on her body. She would inquire about the bruises but the answers she received were always evasive. Seeing Tracey with a black eye, however, forced her to try and get more answers.

"I said, Tracey, you may have terrible luck," Richards recalled. "But nobody is so unlucky that they trip, fall down the stairs, and hit their face on a baseball in the eye socket. So don't give me a lame excuse. You don't have to give me any excuse, but let's take a picture."

Tracey broke down. She gave her friend all of the grisly details, detailing the abuse she suffered at the hands of Hunter. Loran then became her advocate, taking pictures of Tracey's injuries. She would later state that she saw blood stains and other signs of abuse at Tracey's home.

THAT FATEFUL NIGHT

Now divorced, Hunter would arrive at Tracey's home on November 22nd, 2010.

According to Tracey, he then became enraged when Tracey told him that she had spent the night with a new lover.

"He told me that he was gonna kill me," Tracey recalled. Tracey stated that she tried to escape, running into the closet in order to "get away from the kids and to pray." Tracey's eleven-year-old son from a previous relationship was in the home as was the four-year-old daughter they have together.

Hunter caught up with her and knocked her to the ground. He tied a belt around her ankles and then began choking her.

Half-conscious, Tracey alleged to have been raped and sodomized.

The brutal attack would leave Tracey unconscious. She would wake up the next morning on the bathroom floor.

"I called Hunter," Tracey recalled. "I told him that I was bleeding and that I was hurt and that I needed help. And he told me, 'Fuck you. I hope you die."

Tracey wound up in the emergency room after the attack. Hospital records would show that she had a laceration on her head, bruises, and ligature marks on her feet.

Tracey would then be referred to the Turning Point domestic violence center.

Marian Waters would describe Tracey's injuries as among the worst she had ever seen in a twenty-year career.

Waters would testify that Tracey had suffered a horrific assault. She described her mental state as typical of someone who had just been raped; fearful, jumpy, fearing for her life.

Tracey had suffered a hematoma on her side that was the side of a grapefruit. She also claimed to have experienced rectal nerve damage which would require surgery as well as torn vaginal muscles requiring her to have a hysterectomy.

Police were called and Hunter would be arrested for rape, sodomy, kidnapping and domestic violence.

"And at that point, I feared for my life," Tracey recalled. "And I feared for my children's life."

A HIDDEN AGENDA

Hunter would be freed on bail but Tracey got a restraining order against him. She bought a gun and did not go anywhere unarmed.

She took photos of her injuries on the night of the alleged attack and texted them to Loran. Later, they would take more pictures.

Angered, Hunter would stop paying her spousal and child support. Tracey, however, may have had another scenario in mind for obtaining money.

She had forced Hunter to take out a $103,000 life insurance policy around the time their daughter was born.

On May 24, 2012, the day before Tracey shot Hunter, she would place a call to MetLife that was recorded.

"Thank you for calling MetLife, this is Pam. May I please have your name?"

"Tracey Grissom."

Tracey would then explain that she was angry that her husband stopped making payments on his policy. During their divorce proceedings, he had agreed to continue paying the premiums. Tracey stated she was calling to make sure that they had the correct address on file.

"Is there anything else I can do for you today?

"That's gonna be it!" Tracey said, hanging up.

"Well, May 14th was just like any other day," Tracey said, explaining the call to the insurance company. "However, I had moved four different times. Me and my children were running. We were running from Hunter. So I had called the company to let them know that they had my old address and to make an address change."

FALSE RAPE?

Shelly Standridge was hired by Hunter to defend him in the rape case. She would state that Hunter denied raping or even assaulting Tracey that night. Hunter did, however, admit to the fact that he and his wife had consensual sex that night...Rough consensual sex.

"So that night," Standridge said. "Hunter said that she was depressed and claiming she was going to kill herself. She was saying she wanted their relationship to work."

So she undressed in front of him. Her beauty was always impossible for Hunter to resist.

The two had sex despite Hunter having a new girlfriend at home.

Hunter's aunt, Gina, believed that Tracey wanted to kill Hunter before the rape case went to court.

"He had a new girlfriend, he was living with her," Phelps said. "He was moving on with his life. Hunter would claim that Tracey was jealous, obsessive, even stalked them."

"Hunter had moved on," Hunter's aunt said. "There was some court dates coming up that would prove that Hunter was innocent. There were court dates coming up that he would get visitation to his daughter. She had a lot to lose."

Tracey was on the anti-anxiety drug Klonopin. Hunter would tell his attorney that Tracey would take more than her prescribed dose. Because of this, she fell and cut her head. Hunter would then leave the house around 10:30 pm and go to his father's house. Tracey would call him hours later, at 3:20 am.

Hunter would state that Tracey had called to threaten him. She told him if he didn't want the responsibility of the children then she would make it where he would never be able to see them again.

Hunter's attorney did not know what Tracey's motive was for crying rape. She was very upset that he had a girlfriend.

MORE LIES...

Hunter would be arrested nearly twelve hours later, to his total shock.

Tracey would give her side of the story to the police which later is proven to be false.

She would tell police that Hunter had thrown her against the bathtub around 10 pm and claim to be unconscious until 4 am the next morning.

"But her phone records show she was on the phone all night, so she was never unconscious," Standridge said. "She was also using her data at 10:42 that night. She was using it again at 10:50 that night. ... She sends a text to her boyfriend at 1:49 am. She sends a text to her friend at 2:07 am. She sends another text to her boyfriend at 2:07 am."

Tracey would blame the calls on Hunter.

"All I do know is I was not the only person using my phone that night," Tracey said, suggesting that Hunter used her phone.

Medical records would show that Tracey's head wound was "purely superficial".

Only one suture was needed.

Furthermore, there was nothing on the medical record to support the fact that Tracey experienced vaginal and rectal tears. She did have bruises on her ankle and legs but the photos taken by police at the emergency room would not resemble the same photos that Tracey and her friend Loran would take days later. In the photos taken at the emergency room, an area of Tracey's body has no bruises. Days later, there is discoloration.

Tracey's attorney would blame the discrepancy on "blood thinners" which would cause Tracey to bruise easily.

There was also a discrepancy in her phone records. She would take a photo of her inner thigh, a deep bruise. This area of her body was not photographed by police during her emergency room visit. But on December 9th, almost two weeks later, Tracey took a photo of her inner thigh with the deep bruise

"He (Hunter) told me that he would make it to where nobody would ever want me," Tracey said after a 2010 attack. "I didn't report it because I thought he would kill me."

THE FINAL STRAW

Tracey woke up pissed on May 15th, 2012.

Hunter had been ordered to pay $2,100 a month for the rest of his life. He was not complying with the court order claiming that he was "out of work."

Tracey stated that she was on her way to a job interview when she saw a Grissom Construction sign out of the corner of her eye.

She stated that her initial plan was to take a photograph of Hunter at the job site in order to show proof that he was working as part of her litigation.

"I was getting ready to take the picture and when I looked up he was standing almost directly towards the front of the boat trailer," Tracey said. "He was looking back directly at me. He had this face, that's like mean - just, I don't know how to describe it. I mean, I see it over and over like it's right there all the time. He flipped me the bird, which to me was kinda like, 'Yeah I'm workin. Screw you.' And at that point, I panicked. At that point, I didn't know what else to do except to defend myself."

Tracey started firing. The first shot hit Hunter in the arm. He started to run and she fired again repeatedly. One of the bullets punctured Hunter's heart and he died of massive internal bleeding.

William Dockery was working with Hunter and was an eyewitness to the shooting. Hunter had turned to Dockery before the shooting and told him to "call the law". Before Dockery could pick up his cell phone, Tracey had commenced shooting.

Tracey then pulled out her own cell phone and called the cops on herself. She tearfully described that she had just murdered her husband.

CONFESSION

Tracey told detectives exactly what was going through her mind when she came upon Hunter at the construction site.

"Tell me about what happened," the detective said. "What led up to...what's going on."

"In November of 2010, he beat me unconscious and raped me...and, and left me for dead....and, and I finally pressed charges against him and he told me that he would make my life a living hell...and that's what he's done."

"What, what happened this morning that led up to you going..."

"I was going to work and I saw him...and he's been claiming that he-he's not working. And, so I pulled in there to take a picture of him...cause it was the truck that's still in my name...and the boat that's still in my name...and the trailer that's still in my name...He just stared at me and flipped me off...and I just went in there and shot him...I just shot him, I shot him, and I shot him."

Tracey would be distraught and tearful during her interrogation room confession. A few weeks later, however, she would call the insurance company to let them know that Hunter had died.

"Well, I was actually calling because I didn't know what I needed to do ... Hunter passed away May 15th and I actually am going a court case right now because it was due to self-defense..."

Hunter's family went ballistic over this. Tracey would claim that she had no money but she continued to pay his life insurance premiums.

"Even through the times when she's screamin' that she's destitute and has no money ... she continued to pay life insurance premium," Hunter's mother said.

"I don't think my sister concocted a story," Tracey's sister said. "Just so she could get insurance money. ... But that's all they (the prosecution) had."

THE TRIAL

Tracey's allegations of rape and sodomy would not be allowed in court testimony. She was allowed, however, to detail the effects of Hunter's abuse on her were.

Taking the stand, Tracey would lift up her shirt in court and show herself wearing a colostomy bag. She stated that she had undergone several surgeries after her husband's daily rapes wherein she suffered permanent rectal and vaginal damage.

Hunter's family was then allowed to speak at the hearing.

"This tremendous loss has changed me," Hunter's mother, Melanie Garner said. "And I don't know how to change back."

Chloe, Hunter's sister, had a victim's services officer read her letter in court.

"Tracey is psychotic," Chloe wrote. "She is the most selfish person human being on this earth."

"Every mother should pray every night that your son doesn't fall in love with someone like Tracey," Hunter's aunt, Gina Grissom said. "There have been lots of allegations against Hunter. We've never believed anything that has come out of her (Tracey's) mouth."

His aunt then looked directly at Tracey.

"Hunter was proud of his name. Why would you still choose to use our name, and bring it down?" suggesting that if Tracey hated him so much why didn't she go revert to her maiden name after the divorce.

The jurors would find Tracey guilty of murder. She would be sentenced to twenty-five years in prison.

One of the jurors, Janice Kelly, would contact Grissom's attorney Warren Freeman the morning after the trial. She had remorse over her decision and said that she wouldn't have convicted her had they had the rapes and abuse allegations been introduced as evidence.

"I feel I made a mistake," Kelly said. "If I had to do it over again, we'd have had a hung jury. We didn't get her side. She did not get a fair trial."

"We voted to convict because there was no dispute that Tracey shot Hunter," the jury foreman wrote in a letter that was addressed in the courthouse. "Jurors didn't believe prosecutor claims that she did it in order to collect a life insurance policy. We felt the shooting was a crime of passion, not for financial gain and that she should be sentenced accordingly. I wish we had seen evidence of the rape allegation. We feel that she just 'lost it.'"

"It's not fair, it's not fair!" Tracey sobbed as she was led out of the courthouse and to jail.

"We think the sentencing was too harsh," Tracey's attorney Warren Freeman said. "Considering you have the foreperson of the jury actually saying, we don't feel like she should be punished according to being found guilty of murder. Let's just say that there will be a basis for a new trial, and part of it will be something that the jurors saw that they weren't supposed to see and I'm going to just leave it at that until I file my motion."

"My son died running for his life," Hunter's mother said. "I don't know what was running through his mind but I hear him say 'momma.'"

"People who think that I murdered him in cold blood," Tracey said. "Either don't know the whole story or don't know everything that's happened.

Tracey was asked on CBS' 48 hours if she regretted pulling the trigger on that fateful day.

"No," she said flatly. "Because if I hadn't I would be dead. I truly believe that."

"She has a way of making everything she does look right," Hunter's aunt, Gina scoffed.

HUSBAND KILLER DONNA YAKLICH

JESSI DIXO

Old-fashioned police work

In December 1985, a narcotics detective was shot and killed in the driveway of his farm in Pueblo, Colorado, where he lived with his five children and his wife, Donna Yaklich. Initially, authorities suspected Dennis' death was linked to his work in law enforcement, but a tip led them to two teenage shooters – and eventually, back to Dennis' wife, Donna.

However, attorneys for Donna Yaklich argued that Dennis had been beating his wife. The murder, they claimed, was a battered woman's desperate attempt to escape a lifetime of abuse – or potentially becoming a murder victim herself, like Dennis' first wife, who is thought to have died of a diet drug overdose in 1977.

Yaklich was finally acquitted of first-degree murder after a mistrial and a second trial that has been described as "grueling," but was convicted on the charge of conspiracy for hiring gunmen to kill her husband. Her sentence was forty years in prison, but was released to a halfway house in 2005, after serving close to eighteen years.

The young men Yaklich had hired to carry out the murder were also arrested and sentenced. Charles Greenwell, who was only 16 when the crime was committed, received a sentence of twenty years while his brother Eddie, who had been 25, received thirty years.

However, while Yaklich's claims of abuse weren't enough to get her off on the premise of self-defence, they did encourage authorities to reopen their investigation into the death of Barbara Yaklich. According to a cold case team, the investigation was "incomplete."

"This case needed some good, old-fashioned police work," said team lead Steve Johnson, with the Colorado Bureau of Investigation. "In my opinion, I have seen better documented traffic accidents."

Discrepancies were found in the autopsy report, which originally claimed Barbara had fainted from taking diet pills. When her body-builder husband, Dennis, tried "energetically" to resuscitate her, she suffered bleeding in her abdomen. However, administering CPR is not an appropriate reaction to fainting – and as a police officer trained in CPR, Dennis would have known this.

Still, there was apparently no examination of the potential crime scene, and when Dennis was asked to take a polygraph to support his defense, he refused.

Denver-area pathologist Michael Doberson determined that the conclusions in the report were "very unusual" – the internal damage Barbara had suffered, he claimed, was more likely caused by a blow to the abdomen. Doberson included his findings in a letter to Johnson dated in 2005, stating that in his opinion, "the entire scenario is simply not credible." A second forensic pathologist concurred with Doberson's conclusions.

According to reports, Barbara's liver tore open and her abdomen was quickly filled with more than 2,000 millilitres of blood – nearly 40 per cent of her total blood volume, and more than twice as much as is typical in a victim of a fatal car accident.

Investigators are now considering her death as "suspicious," with the tear caused by a blunt force trauma consistent with "punches and knee drops to the upper abdomen," according to pathologist Stephen Cina. However, the autopsy report showed no other indications that would reveal a pattern of abuse – no recorded discoloration, bruising, or external signs of beatings.

While the investigation into Barbara's death is now complete, the case hasn't been closed. According to the coroner and the Pueblo County Sheriff, the public deserves answers to the questions that have been raised.

The family man

Donna Yaklich met Dennis and his children only a few months after Barbara's death. According to Yaklich, the plan was to move in with the family for the summer and help him get the kids back into their home, since they were temporarily staying with Dennis' mother.

"I had no expected to fall in love with the children, who so desperately needed someone," Yaklich said. "They were grieving for their mother, so I couldn't bear to leave them."

Barbara had died on Valentine's Day, and had "appeared fine" as her children left for school that morning. However, an hour later, Barbara was dead – and Dennis was the only person who had been with her as she died. According to some reports, there are members of the community who do continue to question Dennis' involvement in the death of his first wife, including at least one of his former co-workers.

"Dennis' fellow officers knew he was out of control, but they also knew when they needed him he would be the first to go through the door," Yaklich said. "No one who worked with him would go against him."

It was this feeling of hopelessness that eventually led Yaklich to hire gunmen to kill her husband, in an effort to finally end the ongoing abuse. She'd moved in with Dennis when she was only 22 and he was 30. The children were aged 3, 9, 11, and 12 – and she immediately fell into the role of step-mother, despite the abuse which began only a month after Yaklich moved in. She said she attempted to leave a few times, but always went back.

"I feared Dennis, but at the same time I felt at home with him because I had grown up in an abusive environment," Yaklich said. "I fell into the trap of thinking if I could make everything perfect for him, he wouldn't get mad at me or at the kids. Dennis' threats to kill me or kill someone I loved if I ever left again kept me there."

Dennis even threatened to use his access to federal law enforcement agents against Yaklich, telling her that she'd never be able to get away from him – these agents were capable of fiding anyone, anywhere. Eventually, she said, "I lost myself. I lost hope."

"I became very depressed and mad at myself because I had no trusted my instincts about leaving the relationship when the abuse started," Yaklich said. "Suicidal thoughts became an answer. Then came homicidal thoughts."

Looking back, Yaklich admitted that she wished she had listened to those first instincts, but eventually came to a point where she no longer cared. However, she said she has been working on bettering herself since being convicted and sentenced.

"Being in prison is similar to the prison I put myself in while I was married to Dennis," she said. "However, prison is also what you make of it, so I've enrolled in educational programs, had therapy, and also taken care of myself. Things I should have done in society."

A professional abuser

At a menacing 6'5" and 280 pounds, Dennis Yaklich was a competitive weightlifter who continuously used steroids to supplement his workouts – despite the fact that they also enhanced his aggressive tendencies. While the officers who worked with him conceded that he was always the go-to guy for breaking down a door or clearing a room, he was difficult to manage. In fact, when he did become confrontational, even a supervisor threatened to shoot him because they had no other way to defend themselves.

A former partner once stated that he felt he always had to "clean up after Dennis," and other co-workers have admitted they "dreaded" working with Dennis, because of his aggressive and unpredictable behaviour. Some of his closest colleagues have even confessed that

Dennis displayed some "abusive tactics" on the job – while denying the complaints of citizens against him.

Yaklich endured what can only be described as domestic terrorism. While the physical abuse, which included slapping, choking, kicking, and pushing her down stairs as well as sadistic sexual assaults, was indeed disabling and troubling, the psychological abuse was almost worse. According to Yaklich, the threat of death loomed constantly – Dennis would put his gun to her head and threaten to kill her, point his finger at her in the shape of a gun and blow on it after miming shooting her with it, and even beating her under the cover of darkness so she wouldn't be able to prepare for the blows.

The physical abuse has been corroborated by a number of independent witnesses, including a mailman who reported seeing bruises on Yaklich's face, and a telephone repairman who had been called in twice to fix phones after Dennis had yanked them out of the wall in a fit of rage.

Following Yaklich's arrest, the repairman spoke with detectives investigating Dennis' death and said the bruises he had seen on Yaklich's neck and cheek were so prominent, he noticed them "at a glance." The detective inquired how the repairman could recall the incident so vividly, and he admitted that in his line of work, he sees "a lot of things like that in the low income areas and the projects, but I was shocked to see a cop's wife all bruised up like she was."

Cries unheard

Yaklich's first documented attempt for police intervention came in 1982, when she called Dennis' partner to explain that Dennis was "out of control" and threatening to kill her. The detective advised her to leave right away, but she said she was too afraid – if she left, she said, Dennis had told her he would kill her entire family, starting with her father.

Believing that Yaklich was in fear for her life, the detective immediately went to inform his supervisor about the call he'd received about his partner. According to the detective, the supervisor had gestured to indicate that he should just forget the call – it was none of their business – and the incident went unreported.

It was then that Yaklich realized that trying to get help from the police would be completely futile, and she would need to seek support elsewhere.

The next year, in November of 1983, Yaklich endured a short and traumatic visit with a psychologist. After Yaklich "sobbed uncontrollably" through the entire session, the psychologist recommended she leave her husband – but failed to offer her suggestions to muster the courage needed to do so, or what steps she could take to do it safely.

Since Yaklich was required to provide her abusive husband with detailed accounts of where she spent all her time, there was no way for her to continue therapy with regular appointments. She never went back for another session.

A few months later, Yaklich escaped to a battered women's shelter in Denver, in February of 1984. Dennis pleaded with her to come home, and even went so far as to promise that he would try to change – and because she was ashamed to go back to him again, Yaklich told the counselors that she was leaving the state.

Still, the abuse hadn't stopped another year later. Early in 1985, Yaklich tried talking to friends and family members – telling them she needed advice because Dennis was going to kill her. These claims were shrugged off by everyone she turned to, and the abuse began to escalate.

Feeling as though she had no other options, Yaklich began looking for an opportunity to kill herself. Her attempts failed, however, when she realized she would be abandoning her young son and step-children with their abusive father – and after witnessing the struggles of Barbara's children as they grieved the loss of their mother, she was unable to force that situation on her own child.

Later that year, the Pueblo Sheriff's Department received a 911 call from Yaklich's mother. One of the step-children had called Yaklich's parents after hearing what they thought was Dennis pushing Yaklich through a plate glass window. While it turned out that the noise was caused by just a bowl hitting the floor, the officers who responded barely acknowledged Yaklich.

In fact, their inspection of the situation involved a brief conversation with Dennis followed by a tour of the gym Dennis was building on the property. The situation only reinforced Yaklich's desperate situation on the other side of the blue line – living in fear of an abusive spouse with no support or protection from the authorities.

Finally, on December 12, 1985, one of Yaklich's friends finally responded to her pleas for help. A neighbour, Eddie Greenwell, waited at the Yaklich family's farm with his younger brother, Charles, into the early morning hours. When Dennis returned home after working a night shift, the brothers shot and killed him. Yaklich was inside the house, sleeping.

According to court documents, Yaklich had "approached several people" in an attempt to have her husband killed, and had met with Eddie Greenwell many times over a period of eight months. The Greenwell brothers were paid $4,200 in installments after the murder was committed – although the brothers testified they had been promised $45,000.

The story of the tragic marriage was detailed in a made-for-television movie called *Cries Unheard: The Donna Yaklich Story*. The film was released in 1994 and starred former Charlie's Angel Jaclyn Smith as Yaklich.

A disturbing conflict of interest

After Dennis was killed, the Pueblo Police Department – Dennis' employer – carried out an investigation into his death, despite the fact that the murder actually took place in the jurisdiction of the Pueblo

Sheriff's Office. Lead roles in the inquiry were awarded to narcotics detectives – Dennis' partners.

The District Attorney was also a personal friend of Dennis', and even admitted to being a material witness in his own case. At the time of the trial, DA Sandstrom was wrapped up in a highly contested election – and this clear political agenda, combined with the attempts of the police department to hide its role in Yaklich's abuse and ultimately, Dennis' death, indicate incredible prejudice against Yaklich from the very beginning.

Not that Yaklich was surprised. After attempting to secure the help of police several times during the course of her abusive marriage, it was obvious to Yaklich that law enforcement was not on her side.

Still, the jury acquitted Yaklich of the charge of first-degree murder. Several jurors even thought Yaklich deserved to be acquitted of all charges, but felt intimidated by the Pueblo Police Department – and feared potential retaliation. Instead, the jury voted guilty on the charge of conspiracy to commit murder, believing that the fair-minded judge would give the battered wife the minimum sentence of eight years.

The probation supervisor who had conducted Yaklich's pre-sentencing investigation testified that Yaklich would be an "excellent candidate" for sentencing alternatives outside of the Department of Corrections, and gave the court his recommendation for the minimum sentence. His testimony affirmed the sense of desperation Yaklich claimed to be struggling with.

"I really felt that whether they did what she wanted done, to have Dennis killed, or whether Dennis found out and killed her, it didn't matter," he said. "She was at a point in her life where either was satisfactory."

However, the late Judge Seavy who presided over the trial chose to overlook the circumstances leading to Dennis' murder and remanded Yaklich to the Department of Corrections for a sentence of forty years. According to the judge, Yaklich "started this whole scenario," and therefore deserved to serve a period of time "in excess of the longest Greenwell's sentence."

"We cannot overlook the fact that Yaklich's participation in the death of her husband was not merely peripheral," stated court documents. "Had it not been for Yaklich, the Greenwells would not have been involved in this murder. Thus, in our view, we would be establishing poor public policy if Yaklich were to escape punishment by virtue of an unprecedented application of self-defense while the Greenwells were convicted of murder."

Still, the jurors were shocked and horrified by the severity of Judge Seavy's harsh sentence. More than half of the serving jurors submitted letters expressing their disappointment with the resulting sentence to a judge who presided over Yaklich's sentencing reconsideration a few years later. These letters were dismissed by that judge, however, who felt "that they must not allow for personal sympathy to influence their decision." Several of the jurors who served on the initial trial event went on to diligently advocate for Yaklich's early release, eighteen years later.

According to Dr. Lenore Walker, who counseled and evaluated Yaklich and provided expert testimony at her trial, Judge Seavy was "using the court and a woman's life to express his own ignorance of a battered woman's plight."

The conspiracy

According to court documents, Yaklich did receive payments totalling more than $250,000 under her late husband's three life insurance policies – leading to a theory that the motivation that pushed her to arrange her husband's death was to obtain this insurance money. The defense argued that Yaklich suffered from "battered woman syndrome," and that the conspiracy to commit murder was a "justifiable act of self-defence ... committed under duress resulting from years of physical and psychological battering by her husband."

"Yaklich lived in a constant state of fear of her husband," the defense argued. "At the time of his death, she believed she was in imminent danger of being killed by him or receiving great bodily injury from him."

The defense went on to explain that many battered women are unable to safely leave their abusive spouses – and in fact, the abuse often escalates as a result of a separation. Abusers have also been known to pursue their victims after they've left, subjecting them to "brutal attacks."

"Additionally, battered women may not psychologically or emotionally have the alternative of leaving the abuser because of their low self-esteem, their emotional and economic dependency, the absence of another place to go, and the woman's legitimate fear of the abuser's response to her leaving," stated the defense. "Battered women become trapped in their own fear and often feel that their only recourse is to kill the batterer or be killed."

Several people involved with the case, including District Attorney Sandstrom, have stated that if Yaklich had gone ahead and committed the murder herself, "she would have walked." However, the DA and many others also question the validity of Yaklich's testimony, including that Dennis was abusing her – maintaining the theory that Yaklich conspired to have him killed just to receive the insurance money.

The DA even stated that "if she had shot him herself, there would be no issue" – leading some to wonder if Sandstrom sees money as an acceptable motive for murder, as long as you follow through with it on your own.

Like most battered women, Yaklich both loved and hated her husband. Killing him herself would have been difficult, as she was afraid that as soon as she pointed a gun at him to save herself and her children, the love she had for him would "override her fear of him," and cause her to second-guess her decision. The ramifications from that could have bene deadly.

Another concern for Yaklich was her husband's established persona of invincibility – one he had carefully instilled in her over years of repeated psychological and physical abuse. Not only did Yaklich struggle to trust in her own ability to kill her husband, she struggled to believe that he would ever really die.

One of the prosecution's expert witnesses, Dr. Alice Brill, said in her testimony that Yaklich didn't meet the traditional profile of a battered woman. These women, according to Brill, generally kill their spouses with little premeditation and show little interest in pursuing relationships with other men – while Yaklich spent at least ten months planning her husband's murder, and had had at least one extramarital affair about a year before Dennis was killed.

Dennis' children also continue to question Yaklich's testimony, stating that none of them had ever witnessed any physical abuse from Dennis during the eight years of the couple's marriage. After Yaklich's parole hearing in October 2005, Dennis' daughter Vanessa fought back tears while talking about the court's decision to release Yaklich after she'd only served eighteen years of her forty-year sentence.

"It's devastating – I don't believe justice has prevailed," she said. "My father died at age 38. He was stripped of his opportunity to live life. He was prevented from raising his children, from seeing us grow up and accomplishing our goals."

Vanessa stated that Yaklich's claims of beatings and abuse were "an outright lie" – and that the depiction of the family's life shown in the TV-movie *Cries Unheard* were based entirely on prison interviews with Yaklich herself, with no supporting evidence or facts contributed by other relatives or friends.

Vanessa added that just two months before her father was killed, Yaklich had told her that Dennis had asked for a divorce – but that the couple planned to delay the proceedings until after the Christmas holidays, for the sake of the younger children. This story has been corroborated by Dennis' brother, who said Dennis told him over the phone that he planned to divorce Yaklich once the holidays had passed.

"(Dennis') life was taken because he was going to divorce my step-mother and not because she was the victim of abuse," Vanessa said. "I never feared my father, nor did I observe any abuse, whether it be psychological or physical, perpetrated by him. His demeanor was calm and loving, his words encouraging and supportive. I can honestly state my step-mother did not provide my siblings or myself with the same."

According to Vanessa, Yaklich didn't show any grief or remorse after Dennis had been killed – and even slapped Vanessa when she began to cry at her father's funeral. She went on to detail the ongoing "injustice," claiming to defend her father since he is no longer able to defend himself.

"My stepmother's legal defense was paid for by my father's life insurance proceeds and my family and I believe she profited from the made-for-television monstrosity," Vanessa said. "Most recently, her financial status has provided her with the ability to hire a media publicist."

Questions also remain about the relationship Yaklich had with her defense attorney, John Giduck. Records show Giduck and Yaklich took a romantic vacation to Jamaica together prior to her arrest in March 1986 – a getaway funded entirely from the death benefit Yaklich received after having her husband murdered.

In fact, the vacation was cut short when Yaklich was notified of the charges that were being brought against her, and surrendered to police upon her return to Pueblo. Most of the insurance money had already been spent by the time Yaklich was arrested.

According to information reported in the Colorado Springs Gazette, Yaklich had been involved in an extramarital affair about a year before Dennis' murder, and had begun a romantic relationship with Giduck only weeks after her husband's death. Giduck had apparently attended Dennis' funeral, where he had given Yaklich his business card and told him to call if she needed anything.

Yaklich reached out to him a few days later, after police asked her to verify the statement she'd given with a routine polygraph test.

A safe and abuse-free life

Still, Yaklich had a spotless record prior to her incarceration, which continued even after she was sent to prison – a testament to her strength of character. According to prison records, Yaklich managed to vigilantly avoid conflict and strictly followed the many rules surrounding prison life. Despite being forced into an environment filled with trouble, Yaklich managed to stay out of it through her entire eighteen-year term.

During her incarceration, Yaklich obtained an associate's degree as well as a Bachelor's degree in psychology – while working in maintenance and then in a computer-refurbishing program at the correctional facility. According to staff there, Yaklich was a hard and industrious worker, even volunteering her time as a member of the Fire Response Team, comprised of prisoners trained in firefighting and first aid.

Yaklich has also volunteered with several programs that support victims of abuse, earning high praise from her Department of Corrections supervisors regarding the effectiveness of her work with young people. She encourages victims of domestic abuse to seek support from therapy groups to find the strength to break away from an abusive partner – to learn how to stay away emotionally and physically.

"Educating ourselves about the issues and statistics relative to domestic violence will help us pass this information on to the next generation," Yaklich said. "Our children need to learn that they have the right to safe and abuse-free lives."

HUSBAND KILLER : THE TRUE STORY OF KELLY GISSENDANER

68

JENNIFER KENDALL

Kelly Gissendaner, born Kelly Brookshire, became the sixth and last woman executed in Georgia for her role in the murder of her husband, Douglas Gissendaner, by her lover, Greg Owen. The murder was gruesome, Kelly demonstrated a lack of credibility with lies, and the murder was clearly premeditated- three things that helped a jury convict her of her role in the murder. What hurt her the most, though, was that her former lover turned on her and testified against her. Kelly seemingly changed her life in prison, mentoring and preaching to other women. Her legal team appealed the decision due to a lack of proof, her redemption, and her relationship with her children. The mother of three children cried and sang "Amazing Grace" as she received the lethal injection and one hundred people protested her death outside.

Early Life

In 1968, Kelly Brookshire was born to Maxine and Marry Brookshire in Georgia. She has a brother that was born one year after Kelly. Kelly and her brother were not born into wealth or emotional stability. Her family consisted of simple cotton farmers. Her parents drank, did drugs, and fought. Due to the troubled relationship, they did not stay together. Kelly's father left the family and created a new one with no intention of including Kelly into his new family dynamic. This obviously left Kelly feeling unwanted and abandoned. Kelly's mother did remarry a man named Billy Wade eight days after the divorce with Kelly's father was final, but Billy only added more trauma to Kelly's already broken home. Many people came forward with knowledge of sexual abuse to Kelly by her stepfather and other men. On top of the sexual abuse, Billy Wade was physically and emotionally abusive to Kelly, her brother, and her mother. Luckily, her mother also divorced Billy Wade and moved the family.

Kelly stood at six feet tall, and she was rather homely looking. Many people made fun of her for her looks and being "trailer trash". She would prefer to work rather than socialize, mostly due to her household's financial situation and her mother's strict rules. Her first job was at McDonald's. She mostly kept to herself, but the outcast made one friend in a woman named Mitzi.

First child and marriage

Kelly got pregnant with her first child before she finished high school. She claimed that the child was conceived through date rape, and the father was not actively involved in the child's life. She refused to name the father to even her best friends. She also tried to hide the pregnancy for as long as she could, but the reality became apparent around her sixth month. Before she gave birth, her father reached out to her and suggested that she name the child with his last name. Her first child, Brandon Brookshire, was born in June of 1986. Kelly married her first husband, Jeff Banks, at the young age of nineteen, but the marriage only lasted for six months before it dissolved. Reports indicate that the marriage quickly ended when Kelly's father threatened Jeff with a gun for not passing him bread at the dinner table. After the marriage ended, Kelly and her baby moved into her mother's trailer. This was a rough time for Kelly, but she was saved when she met Douglas Gissendaner.

Marriage to Douglas Gissendaner

On September 2, 1989, Kelly became Mrs. Douglas Gissendaner... for the first time. Kelly was four months pregnant on her wedding day, which could have encouraged the nuptials. The marriage was tumultuous from the beginning. They had financial difficulty after they both lost their jobs and were forced to live with Doug's parents for some time. However, Doug provided a good life for Kelly and her child when he decided to enlist in the United States Army. Despite a steady paycheck, Kelly used the money irresponsibly and needed Doug's family to help her with car payments. Doug's parents already didn't love Kelly, and this added to their distrust. When Doug moved to Germany because of his job in the army, it only added to the tension. The move happened only one month after Kelly had given birth to their first child together and her second child, Kayla. When Kelly and Doug were together, they were noticeably miserable. The relationship did not work at all, and they fought constantly. People also spoke up about Kelly's partying and sleeping around with other men while Doug wasn't around. This caused even more strain on the family, and the couple divorced in 1993. This time, Kelly joined the army with no other way to support herself and her children, but she discovered that she was not made for the army. During this time, Kelly became pregnant with another man and gave birth to her final child Jonathan who everyone called Cody. This father would die of cancer shortly after his birth. After returning from the army, Kelly and Doug reconciled. Despite having a child with another man, they didn't want to separate their family. They remarried in May of 1995 and, despite a separation during this time, bought a house together in Auburn, Georgia in December of 1996. A few months later, Doug was murdered.

Greg Owen

While divorced from Doug, Kelly started working for the International Readers League of Atlanta. At this time, she started socializing with her boss, Belinda Owens. When she met Belinda's brother Greg Owen, they had an instant chemistry. The relationship started strong, but it soon started to worry Belinda. Belinda noticed an alarming amount of fighting, and she didn't appreciate the bossy tone that Kelly used when she spoke to her brother. Kelly and Greg broke up, and Kelly went back to Doug and remarried. Kelly and Greg rekindled their romance during a brief separation between Kelly and Douglas, but Kelly ultimately stayed married to Douglas. Many suspect her devotion to her relationship with Doug involved stability for her and her children rather than love. This was only amplified by the fact that many reports indicated that she continued to maintain a relationship with Owen throughout her marriage to Douglas.

Murder and Investigation

In February 7, 1997, Douglas Gissendaner was murdered by in a secluded part of rural Gwinnett County. Douglas came home from a friend's house shocked to find Gregory Owen in his home. Gregory then exhibited a knife and forced Douglas to drive to a remote area. When they stopped, Owen forced Douglas out of the car and made him walk 300 feet into the woods before beating him in the skull with a nightstick and repeatedly stabbing him in the neck and back. When Kelly arrived, she helped set the car on fire to eliminate any evidence.

The night of the murder, Kelly had gone out for dinner and drinks with friends. Despite dancing and having a good time, she went home right around midnight. Friends with her that night reported that she told them that she went home because she had a feeling that there was something wrong. Kelly frantically searched for Doug when he didn't come home the next day. She made several calls, but she reportedly could not locate him. She even called his parents to ask if they had seen him. That same day a missing person's report was created by the local police department, and they started their search immediately.

Investigators had trouble with Kelly's story from the start. When she spoke with them, she described her marriage as happy and noneventful, but other people provided reports of fighting and numerous problems including Kelly's infidelity. One name that came up over and over again in interviews with friends and family was Greg Owen.

Greg Owen seemed to have a reasonable alibi. A roommate stated that he was home all night and got picked up by a friend for work the following morning at 9:00 a.m. With his roommate's alibi, police put Greg's interrogation on hold and continued their investigation.

Investigators finally got a big clue when they found Doug's car. It was left on a rural road in Gwinnett County. The most interesting thing about finding the car was that it appeared to be burned from the inside. At this time, there was no sign of Doug. While the situation didn't look good for Doug, family and friends knew that police were getting closer to the truth.

The day that the car was found, friends and family gathered to the home of Doug Sr. and Sue Gissendaner to support them during this difficult time. Kelly made an appearance, but she didn't stay long. She decided instead to take her children to the circus. While some people can understand how the environment can be traumatic to the children and maybe Kelly wanted to protect them, people found her decision evasive and questionable. Also, shouldn't the children be allowed to mourn with their grandparents? To increase suspicion even more, Kelly went back to work only four days into the search for her missing husband. Her behavior confused people around her. Sure, she had bills to pay, but four days was very soon to go back to work. Many people thought that she was hiding something. Many more people reported a weird attitude for a woman who had a missing husband.

After an already excruciating twelve days for Doug's friends and family, Doug's body was finally found in a horrific condition a mile from where they had found his car. His body appeared to be a bag of trash at first. He was on his knees, bent over, with his face in the dirt. Twelve days of decomposition, the elements, and animal attacks made him virtually unrecognizable. Medical professionals used dental records to confirm that the body was indeed Doug Gissendaner. He had been stabbed four times in the head, neck, and back.

While there was a long list of potential suspects, investigators kept Kelly close. When they talked to her again to go over her initial statements, the pressure must have gotten to her. She finally admitted that she had spoken to Greg on occasion when he called her. She made it clear to police that she did not pursue any relationship with Greg, and he pursued her. She also admitted that she reconciled with Owen during a separation, and she told investigators that he said that he would kill Doug when he found that she was getting back together with him. At this time, she pointed the finger at Greg and police questioned him heavily. Their relationship was officially over.

With the investigation focused on Greg, Greg's roommate changed his story completely. He was afraid that his leis could get him in trouble, and he told the police a new story. In fact, he confessed to investigators that Greg had been gone the night before until 8 am the next morning. With Greg's alibi gone, investigators knew they were getting even closer to the truth.

Kelly's story was raveling apart as well when investigators pulled up phone records that showed 47 calls between the two. They also saw that Kelly initiated the calls 18 times, which goes against what she told them while interrogated that she only spoke to him because he constantly called her. Furthermore, the correspondence ended immediately after the murder. Why would they stop talking so suddenly for no reason? Her inconsistencies made her look bad to the investigators who were suspicious of her story from the beginning.

After more interrogation, Greg confessed to the murder after he was told that cooperation could prevent him from getting the death penalty. He proceeds to implicate Kelly to save himself. He explains how he and Kelly had an intimate relationship, and she told Greg that she wanted him to kill Doug after they settled into their new house. She even came up with alibis at this time. He goes on to describe the murder in detail. He stated that Kelly picked him up and allowed her into his house. She even gave him the nightstick and the knife that he would use to attack her husband. She advised him to make it look like a home invasion and robbery. Greg waited until Doug got home at around 11 pm, and then he forced him to drive out to the boondocks by knifepoint. They eventually stopped, and Greg forced Doug out of the car and told him to walk. He committed the horrible murder by hitting him in the head with the nightstick and then stabbing him repeatedly, leaving him to bleed. Once completed, Kelly arrived with kerosene to get rid of the evidence. After the murder, Kelly told Greg that they shouldn't speak anymore until things die down. This is the confession that Greg gave police. With this confession, Greg only received a sentence of twenty five years to life instead of the death penalty.

As soon as the police had Greg's confession, they went to also arrest Kelly. They barged into her home on February 25th and completed the arrest. Kelly changed her story once again after her arrest. She confessed that she saw Greg Owen the night of the murder. This time she said that he called her, and she went to pick him up. When he picked her up, he told her about the murder. He then proceeded to threated to murder her and her children as well if she did not help him. Even though the police didn't believe her, Kelly maintained her innocence. Greg was only lying to save himself! She even turned down the plea deal offered to her and decided to go to trial. It was the same plea deal that the prosecution gave Greg- a guilty plea would give her twenty five to life, but she would not get the death penalty. Even her lawyer suggested that she take the plea deal, but Kelly decided to go to trial.

Trial

The first day of Kelly's trial was on November 2, 1998. The jury consisted of two men and ten women. Reporters were prevalent throughout the proceedings.

Prosecutors started by painting a picture of a troubled marriage between Kelly and Doug and her affair with Greg Owen. They then claimed that Gissendaner killed her husband to receive the house he bought for the family and two $10,000 life insurance policies. The reward was surprisingly small but substantial enough to be considered a motive alongside her affair. Prosecution also pointed out inconsistencies in her police reports of the night and the fact that Kelly specifically waited until Doug had bought the house for her and her children. She even had the foresight to plan alibis. This indicated that the murder was premeditated.

The prosecution brought many people into court to testify against Kelly. She faced her late husband's father, who was a witness in her trial. He brought up the troubled marriage between Kelly and his murdered son as well as her questionable relationship with Greg. While many people tried to argue that Doug Sr. already disliked Kelly, his closeness to the situation proved effective.

Another witness was Laura McDuffie. Laura McDuffie was an inmate who was in jail with Kelly. While the defense pointed out that the convict may not be the most trustworthy source and McDuffie only wanted time off of her sentence, her claims were convincing. McDuffie confessed that Kelly offered her $10,000 to take the fall for the murder of Doug Gissendaner. Kelly went so far as to provide a map and a handwritten statement of what McDuffie should say. A handwriting expert confirmed that the statement was in fact written by Kelly.

Kelly's own friend Pam was a witness for the prosecution, too. Pam told the jury that Kelly called her and told her that she had killed Doug. She called back at a later time and said that Greg had forced her to do it by threatening to kill her and her children. Pam claimed that Kelly said, "I did it," but the defense claimed that pam heard incorrectly. Other friends also stepped up to voice they're uneasiness with her behavior while her husband was missing.

The strongest witness for the prosecution, though, was Greg Owen. His statement matched very closely with his confession, but there were certain differences that poked holes in his statement. He originally said that he drove for some time and then Kelly arrived when Doug was dead. He changed the time that Kelly showed up to the murder scene as he was finishing murdering Doug. Doug originally stated that he and Kelly burned the car together, but he then changed his story to say that Kelly simply threw a bottle of kerosene out of the window for him and he burned the car alone. Even with some holes in his original story, the confession remained very damning for Kelly. The former lovers found themselves implicating each other in their once common scheme.

The defense stated that the prosecution could not prove Kelly's innocence beyond a reasonable doubt. Furthermore, Doug Gissendaner was significantly larger than Greg and was also trained by the military. It seemed unreasonable that Doug would obey Greg's commands even if he did have a knife. Greg showed no sign of injury or struggle. It also didn't seem fair that Greg only got a life sentence when he was the one who committed the murder. Also, Greg's testimony, which was part of a plea bargain, gave him incentive to implicate Kelly for a lower sentence for himself.

In the end, a trial of her peers found Kelly Gissendaner guilty after deliberating for only two hours and sentenced her to the death penalty. In just a couple of words, Kelly's life came to an end. However, she was going to do whatever she could to save herself.

Life in Prison

Kelly was taken to prison where she was the only woman on death row. Being on death row, Kelly did her best to retain a relationship with her three children. She also continued to appeal her case, focus on her spiritual health, and mentor other prisoners.

While on death row, Kelly could not socialize with the general prison population. However, she could preach and act as a spiritual guide by talking to inmates through a vent. Mrs. Gissendaner created a bit of a name for herself in prison, and the women inmates supported her throughout her trial. They even called themselves the Struggle Sisters and rallied for her to be taken off of death row and allowed to live the rest of her life in prison.

Execution Reschedules

Her actual execution was actually the third time that Gissendaner had been scheduled for execution. She was previously scheduled for execution at the end of February, but the date was changed due to complications with winter weather. Next, she was scheduled for execution in the first week of March, but the doctors at the prison were concerned because the drug used to perform the lethal injection appeared cloudy. They sent a specimen to be tested, and, in April, they announced the results that there was nothing wrong. Gissenander's lawyers tried claiming that the changes in her execution date constituted cruel and unusual treatment, but the case was thrown out. If anything, Kelly was given more time, but her lawyers fought to the end.

Death

It was 12:21 a.m. on a Wednesday morning in Jackson, Georgia when officials declared Kelly MN Gissendaner dead from lethal injection. Her execution was scheduled for 7:00 p.m., but her lawyers attempted to repeal the decision to the very end. One hundred people stood outside of the Georgia Diagnostic and Classification Center in protest of her death. Her last meal was nachos, chips with cheese dip, and frozen lemonade.

Gissendaner showed remorse for her part in her ex-husband's death until the very end. Her last words were, "Bless you all. Tell the Gissendaners I am so, so sorry that an amazing man lost his life because of me. If I could take it all back, I would." Her words can be interpreted to indicate a sense of guilt on Gissendaner's part. It can also be interpreted to indicate a peace with her position.

Kelly Gissendaner was the only woman at death row for the entire duration of her time incarcerated, and she was the first woman to be given the death penalty in Georgia since 1945- over 70 years. She was one of only six women executed in the state, and she was the last woman to be executed in Georgia.

Appeals and Support

Kelly's lawyers made a valiant attempt at an appeal. In fact, the appeal was more than fifty pages when they turned it in, and it had statements from a number of different people, including inmates, the pope, and political figures.

After being approached by Mrs. Gissendaner's lawyer, the pope responded in a letter stating, "While not wishing to minimize the gravity of the crime for which Ms. Gissendaner has been convicted, and while sympathizing with the victims, I nonetheless implore you, in consideration of the reasons that have been presented to your Board, to commute the sentence to one that would better express both justice and mercy."

The endorsement by the pope was powerful, but the Catholic Church had also just recently vocalized a stance against the death penalty. Even former Georgia Supreme Court Chief Justice Norman Fletcher stood up for the defendant saying that her role in the murder did not constitute the death penalty. In addition to these endorsements, 90,000 people also signed a petition to support Kelly. Kelly's lawyers showed the courts that Kelly showed remorse and represented a criminal who had turned her life around to bring positivity to those around her. They argued that her presence was significantly greater than her absence to those around her, especially her children and other inmates.

Mrs. Gissendaner's lawyers attempted three appeals to the U.S. Supreme Court, but they were denied all three times. Unfortunately, on the day of the execution, Mrs. Gissendaner's children had to choose between saying good-bye to their mother or appearing in front of a judge for one last attempt to appeal her case. The last time that they saw their mother was two days earlier on Monday. In the most heartbreaking of all testimonies, Kelly's daughter, Kayla pleaded with the court to save her mother's life. She made the point that she had already lost her dad, and he would not want her or her siblings to endure any further loss by also losing their mother. Despite the emotional appear and strong endorsements, the court did not waver on its original decision.

Despite the support from multiple sources, Douglas's family, especially his father, maintained throughout the trial that they trusted the legal system and agreed with the sentence of the death penalty. They reminded the public that she chose to go to trial instead of pleading guilty. They also reminded the public that Douglas did not get any choice in what happened to his life. After the gruesome death of their son, an exhausting and emotional search for the truth, and a prolonged trial, Douglas Gissendaner Sr. and Sue Gissendaner got justice.

Death Penalty Debate

Kelly Gissendaner's case became famous across the nation because of its legal implications regarding the death penalty. People for the death penalty noted that Kelly had orchestrated the entire murder, she helped dispose of the body, she lied multiple times, and the family of Douglas Gissendaner deserved justice. People opposed to the death penalty noted that there was room for doubt, she technically did not commit the murder, the person who did commit the murder escaped the death penalty, she showed remorse over her part in the murder, she experienced trauma in her childhood, and she regularly preached and encouraged other women in the prison. Men and women all over the country debated the case, but, ultimately, the death penalty ruling was honored by the state of Georgia, and Kelly was executed while she sobbed and sang "Amazing Grace". She was 47-years-old.

WENDI ANDRIANO

Chapter 1

A dying husband needs a devoted wife. But when love runs out, marriage becomes a burden.

On October 8, 2000, Wendi Andriano snapped. She had played the part of devoted wife to her terminally ill husband, Joe Andriano, for years, but when the love left their marriage, so did Wendi's patience for her husband's eventual demise.

Wendi had a plan to help nudge nature along, and when her plan b expired, she took matters directly into her own hands and bludgeoned him to death.

Wendi first tried to poison her husband by spiking his last meal, a homemade beef stew, with sodium azide, but Joe Andriano did not ingest enough to kill him, only enough to vomit it back up. Wendi then grabbed the nearest object, a bar stool, and beat her dying husband over the head so many times that parts of his brain became exposed.

After thinking she had successfully killed her husband twice, Wendi then realized that Joe was still breathing, so she took a knife from the family kitchen and stabbed him in the side of the throat.

Minutes later, Joe was finally dead.

This bizarre and frantic way Wendi killed her husband isn't the strangest thing about the case though. Known even to Wendi, Joe was due to die from terminal cancer within the next few years anyways.

Why Wendi couldn't wait to kill her husband is an intriguing tale wrought with sex, lies, and strangely, a lack of patience.

Chapter 2

Wendi and Joe Andriano grew up together in the small farming community of Casa Grande, Arizona. But while they both had gone to the same school, they never dated. As a minister's daughter, Wendi's social life was restricted to her father's church. Her celebration for graduating high school was even in the form of a missionary trip to

Mexico in 1989. When she returned she took a job at the local clerical hospital.

Wendi met Joe in 1992 through friends. Although when the couple started dating Joe's family found the minister's daughter to be an unusual fit for the loud, outgoing former football player, they all thought she was friendly enough and approved of the match.

Joe worked for a local boat builder. He was very mechanically inclined and was a very good welder. He owned his own boat and took Wendi for several cruises around the local hot spots for speedboats. They were inseparable.

The couple married in January of 1994. Their wedding took place in a baptist church across the street from their shared elementary school. Their reception was at the Elk's club and was populated by their many friends and family. Even after two years of dating, though, Joe's family felt like they didn't know his new bride very well, but Joe seemed to be very happy, so they were happy for him.

Soon after marrying, the couple became business partners when they started a small company that did windshield repair and replacement. The business combined Wendi's office experience with Joe's mechanical experience, skills they both exceeded at, and the business thrived.

The couple hadn't been married a whole year yet before they faced their first major challenge together. That fall, Joe noticed an odd bump on his neck. When he had it tested, he was told it was a non-cancerous benign tumor, but it wasn't long before they were second-guessing the diagnoses. A year after it was removed, the tumor grew back.

A second surgery and round of tests seemed to reconfirm that the tumor was benign, but shortly after Wendi gave birth to a son in 1997, the tumor was back yet again.

The third time the tumor returned, Joe's wife and family were convinced that the tumor had to be cancer. This fear was confirmed in 1998 when Joe underwent surgery to have the bump removed for the fourth time. Joe's pre-surgery chest x-ray showed that not only was the tumor cancerous, but that the cancer had now spread across Joe's throat, chest, and lungs.

The prognosis wasn't good—Joe had a rare form of cancer and while radiation and chemotherapy were standard, there was no guarantee they would work. On top of this, Wendi was also pregnant again and was only months away from giving birth to the couple's second child.

Chapter 3

In an effort to increase Joe's chances of survival while decreasing his suffering, Wendi and Joe decided to pursue holistic treatments before resorting to chemotherapy and radiation. They had been told that chemotherapy and radiation treatments would likely not cure Joe, but they would lengthen his life by a few years; however, these years would be anything from pleasant. The horrific side-effects chemotherapy and radiation treatments cause are well known.

So the Andriano's decided first to try anything from special diets to alternative medical treatments to prayer—anything that had a chance to help Joe. Joe even attended a holistic treatment centre for cancer patients in Colorado for a few weeks where he was surrounded by other men and women facing the same prognosis as him. After seeing the bravery of others in the same position as him, Joe began thinking about his future again and began to see it as bright for the first time in a while.

After Joe returned from his holistic healing getaway with a bright new attitude, the Andriano's decided the next best step would be for Joe to begin chemotherapy treatments. He had begun to crave his future and was ready to take steps to achieve it. Unfortunately, taking these steps meant that Joe needed to quit his welding job as well as his own position in the couple's business.

To help make ends meet, Wendi returned to working for the first time since the birth of the couple's children. She ended up taking multiple jobs and worked long hours while continuing to care for her husband at home. Eventually, Wendi landed a job managing the San Riva apartment complex in the Ahwatukee foothills, an upscale neighbourhood outside of Phoenix.

Wendi's new job came with some major perks—the salary was above average, which was nice as Wendi was now the family's breadwinner, and it required Wendi to live on site, which meant that the family now lived in a luxury apartment but paid no rent. Wendi's new job also gave her a new life. A large part of her duties as complex manager was arranging social activities for the other residents of the San Riva apartments, who were mostly young, wealthy, single businesspeople.

Every Saturday the complex hosted picnics, pool parties, or late-night socials. The residents even had their own baseball team. Wendi was required to attend every event, which meant Joe was needed to stay home with their two children. Wendi enjoyed this alone time so much that many of the residents at the San Riva had no clue she had a dying husband and two children at home. She partied like she was single.

The first few months at the San Riva went well. Wendi organized mixers and pool parties for the tenants while Joe took care of the kids. Despite being very weak from treatments, he did everything he could, he wanted to do it. He prefered to have his kids around him even when he didn't feel good.

Although they had never gotten close to their daughter-in-law, Joe's parents also pitched in with babysitting so the couple could have time alone together. They didn't get to see each other much as Wendi began spending more and more time at work. Her new job had also given her a new confidence, and she spent many nights out on the town dancing and drinking away her weekday stress with friends. Joe began to fear that Wendi would soon leave him for her new lifestyle, but this fear got sidetracked when his health continued to fail.

In the summer of 2000, when tests revealed his cancer had spread yet again, Joe and Wendi decided to increase the frequency of Joe's chemotherapy. Joe agreed to undergo more treatments, but they quickly took their toll. He lost 15 pounds in the first week alone, and Joe's doctor became concerned. It went from bad to worse very quickly.

By the beginning of October 2000, it became harder and harder to remain optimistic about Joe's chances of beating his cancer. It became apparent it was terminal, but doctors insisted that with treatment Joe could live for several more years.

No one had any idea that Joe would be dead after only the first week of the month. No one, that is, except for one person—Wendi Andriano.

Chapter 4

Just after 2:00 a.m. on October 8, Wendi Andriano called a friend who also lived in the San Riva apartment complex. She told her friend that she needed someone to stay with the kids while she took Joe to the hospital. When the friend arrived, she found Joe on the floor, barely alive.

Joe was on the floor in the fetal position. There was vomit on the floor around him and he couldn't stand up. Wendi confided in her friend that she told Joe that she had called 9-1-1 and paramedics were on the way, but this wasn't true. After seeing Joe in such poor condition, the neighbour urged Wendi to call paramedics. She then went outside to wait for them to arrive while Wendi waiting with her husband.

Wendi did call 9-1-1, but when the EMT's arrived minutes later, she refused to let them or her friend inside the apartment. She said that her husband was dying from terminal cancer and had a do not resuscitate order. Joe was not to receive any medical attention.

Just over an hour later, at 3:30 a.m., Wendi dialed 9-1-1 a second time. The same team of paramedics came to the house. It didn't take them long to realize something wasn't quite right, so they contacted the police department. Both the paramedics and the police were shocked to find out that Joe, who had been terminally ill from cancer for quite some time had died, but not from the cancer that had been slowly killing his body. He died from being repeatedly beaten with a bar stool and from being stabbed in the neck.

When the police opened the front door of the apartment, they were confronted with obvious signs of a deadly struggle. The apartment was in a complete state of disarray, and there was blood everywhere. Blood had been traced throughout the kitchen, the dining room, and the living room of the luxury apartment, and blood had spattered across the walls the ceilings. Lying in the middle of the bloody scene was Joe, with a knife wound in his neck and holes spattered across his visible skull.

While crime scene technicians surveyed the apartment, phoenix police took Wendi down to the station for a formal statement. She was wearing clothes drenched in Joe's blood and was armed with a story that explained how Joe's death had been a complete accident.

In the interrogation room, Wendi told police she and joe had spent the evening in Casa Grande visiting with Joe's parents. They put the kids to bed after they returned home, which was when Joe noticed something odd about Wendi's appearance—she wasn't wearing her wedding ring.

According to Wendi, Joe worked himself into a rage and began accusing her of having an affair. This argument turned into a shoving match, and when Joe grabbed a belt, Wendi grabbed a bar stool and swung. Joe went down on all fours so she hit him again. It was then that she called her neighbour for help. Joe may have been in a terrible state when the neighbour saw him, but according to Wendi when she went outside Joe had gotten back to his feet easily.

Wendi said she denied the EMTs access to the apartment because she and Joe were both embarrassed about the fight, but just minutes after the EMTs left, the fight got physical again.

Wendi said that her husband tried to strangle her with a telephone cord and she defended herself with the first weapon she could get in her hands—a kitchen knife. She was vague about how the knife ended up in Joe's neck though, saying she was holding the knife up when Joe suddenly fell flat on his face. The next thing she knew, blood was spurting everywhere. He must have fallen on the blade, it was simply an accident.

Many things about this story didn't make sense to the police. First of all, the timeline presented in Wendi's story didn't match the accounts of Wendi's neighbour or the EMTs. Wendi's neighbour had seen no evidence of a physical fight when they first entered the apartment—there were no broken bar stools or blood like later when the police arrived. As well, Wendi had few injuries on her body, definitely no injuries that would necessitate self defence in the form of murder.

Joe's illness also shed doubt on Wendi's story. Joe's parents told police that when the Andriano's visited earlier that evening, Joe had been so weak from his treatments that he could barely stand. They had spent the evening doting on their sick son, bringing him any comforts he wanted. If he was too weak to stand, he certainly couldn't have been strong enough to violently attack Wendi.

Police also uncovered a damning piece of evidence from Wendi herself, in a moment when she thought she was all alone. The investigators that had been questioning Wendi left her on her own in the interrogation room for some time while they fact checked some of her statements and checked in with the investigators who were scanning the crime scene for evidence. During this time, Wendi made a phone call to a coworker at the apartment complex and asked them to hide some of her files from the police. This immediately led to a search of Wendi's office where police found evidence that Wendi had in fact killed her husband. She had even been planning it for months.

Chapter 5

While both investigators strongly believed that Wendi Andriano was responsible for Joe's death, they were stumped by her motive. Why would Wendi kill her dying husband? The police didn't know, but they did have one intriguing lead—the phone call Wendi had made from the interrogation room. They were determined to find out what she was trying to hide.

When they searched her office, police discovered that Wendi had been disciplined at work for using her computer to search inappropriate items on the internet while on the clock.She had been conducting research on poisons, and how to use certain poisons to kill people. They also discovered the papers that she had tried to hide—shipping notices for a substance known as sodium azide.

Sodium azide is a lethal substance with a variety of industrial uses including propelling airbags. It is not, however, something that the average person can simply go out and buy. It's not restricted to the point where only certain companies can possess it, but it needs to be bought for a reason—something that an apartment complex didn't have. But based on the information on the shipping invoice, Wendi had found a way around that.

Wendi had created a fictitious business license using the tax ID form for the apartment complex. Using a Xerox machine and an exacto knife, Wendi had removed all information specific to the apartment complex and inserted fictitious information for a fake company.

The business name on the shipping notice was bogus, but the address wasn't. Wendi had the substance delivered to an address in Scottsdale, Arizona in an attempt to distance herself, but that plan didn't work. When the police tracked down the real address on the invoice, workers at the company positively identified Wendi as the person who had come by a couple weeks earlier to pick up a package she had mistakenly had shipped there instead of her own office.

Wendi's coworkers had seen her with a package but that she had been very mysterious with the contents. She refused to tell anyone what was inside. Had this been the sodium azide? And if so, where was it now?

Chapter 6

Suspecting that Wendi had tried to poison Joe with the sodium azide, police took samples of every medication and food they could find in the Andriano's apartment. If Joe had ingested poison, it would have explained the awful state Wendi's friend had seen him in just over an hour before he died. Luckily, the remainders of Joe's last supper, homemade beef stew, still sat in a pot on the stove.

However, police didn't find any evidence of Wendi's mysterious package, or any evidence of the sodium azide itself in Wendi and Joe's apartment. They had just begun to lose hope in finding the poison when they found out Wendi had a storage space in the building that she failed to tell the police about. Hidden behind a stack of boxes in Wendi's storage unit was a small bottle of white powder and a measuring spoon. The white powder was soon identified as sodium azide.

But the storage unit wasn't the only place investigators found the lethal substance—it was also in Joe's stomach contents and in the beef stew on the stove.

While discovering the poison helped police understand that Wendi had been trying to kill her husband, it didn't explain why she had bludgeoned him to death on October 8, 2000. Wendi had spent a lot of time researching poisons and she spent a lot of time manufacturing documents so that she could purchase the poison. It certainly wasn't a spur of the moment decision.

But why would Wendi beat and stab her husband if she had already poisoned him? Prosecutors had a theory, one that would cut to the heart of the crime. It was patience—or more precisely, Wendi's lack of it—that had killed Joe in the end.

Wendi had grown tired of waiting for the cancer to kill Joe, so she decided to give nature a little nudge by poisoning his supper. But according to the theory, when Wendi gave Joe the poison, things didn't go quite to plan. Joe hadn't ingested enough poison to kill him when he began vomiting it back up. With her plan quickly failing, Wendi panicked. She snapped.

Now improvising, Wendi beat Joe with the nearest object she could get her hands on—a bar stool. Pathologists were able to conclude that Wendi beat Joe over the head with the stool no less than twenty-four times. This beating did render Joe unconscious, but still didn't kill him so Wendi grabbed a kitchen knife and stabbed him in the part of his body that caused all this trouble in the first place—the side of his neck.

Chapter 7

Ten days after she murdered her husband, Wendi Andriano was formally charged with first degree murder. Wendi's crime was viewed as being especially cruel due to the large amount of suffering Joe had had to endure over several hours thanks to Wendi's actions. Because of this, the prosecutor's on Wendi's trial did the almost unthinkable, they sought the death penalty.

When Wendi a walked into the Arizona courtroom on September 9, 2004 she looked vastly different from the perky apartment manager that the residents of the San Riva apartments used to know.

At the time of the killing she had been blonde, she had short hair, and generally appeared to be much younger and cute than the individual who appeared in court with long dark hair and thick glasses. Previously, she had liked to look good and show her figure so her conservative dress at the trial was certainly different from the look her friends were used to seeing. She was trying to look more conservative, more innocent.

She had had plenty of time to perfect her new look—it had taken prosecutors almost four years to bring the case to trial. It had been postponed about 12 times before it was finally brought before a judge and jury.

In their opening statement, prosecutors reminded the jury that at the time of the murder Wendi had been anything but the perfect mother or wife she claimed to have been. She had been someone who had no disregard for her husband at all. While her husband was dying, she had gone out partying and started affairs, and when his condition worsened, and it began to cramp her style, she turned to poison.

Wendi didn't like her new role as family breadwinner, especially with the loss of Joe's income, and with rising medical bills, the family was in the worst financial state they had ever been in. Wendi had thought she was going to be able to be a stay-at-home-mom for the rest of her life, and she did not adjust well to her return to the workforce. So Wendi had found an out.

Although Joe did not have any life insurance, even though Wendi had asked several friends to pretend to be Joe in medical exams so he could be insured, Joe had filed a malpractice suit against his former doctor who had continually told him his tumor was benign when it was in fact spreading throughout his body. If Joe died and the lawsuit went through, Wendi would likely walk away with a multi-million dollar settlement.

More than money though, Wendi had wanted freedom. She wanted the freedom to be single again, she wanted freedom to the ball-and-chain who was slowly dragging her spirit into his grave along with himself. Wendi wanted to not have to care about her dying husband anymore, who was too weak to provide her with any love.

Wendi maintained her plea of innocence throughout the trial, and her defence team attempted to prove she had been the victim of abuse not only on the night of Joe's death but also throughout the couple's entire marriage. To explain the poison, Wendi told the court that Joe had been the one who had grown tired of waiting for the cancer to end his life, and had asked Wendi to help him do it himself.

On the witness stand Wendi said that Joe had willingly taken the poison, but she also stuck by the story that she had originally told police, that Joe had suspected an affair and became enraged when she affirmed them. He became deranged and attacked her, starting the bloody fight. Wendi claimed Joe had died during the ensuing struggle.

Wendi's story wasn't enough to convince the court though, and on November 18, 2004 she was found guilty of the crime. It had taken the jury only two-and-a-half-hours to come to its unanimous decision. Six years after her husband joe had been diagnosed with terminal cancer, Wendi Andriano faced a possible death sentence of her own.

On December 20, 2004, the jurors assigned to Wendi Andriano's case met and decided on Wendi's fate—it would be death for Ms Andriano. Wendi, along with most of the courtroom, was aghast. Even Joe's family was shocked by the decision. Wendi Andriano became the second ever woman to be put on death row in Arizona, a state that reserves the death penalty for the worst of the worst.

Wendi Andriano has since attempted to appeal the court's decision, but as of early 2017, all attempts have been denied and Wendi continues to wait on death row. Wendi and Joe's children now live with Joe's parents, who continue to mourn the loss of their beloved son.

Joe Andriano's death was especially long, and especially cruel, but no happy ending was found when Wendi was sentenced to her own death. Many view the conclusion of this case to be the saddest possible outcome. On October 8, 2000, two lives were lost, and two children were left without parents.

INSTANT MESSAGE MURDERER : THE TRUE STORY OF SHAREE MILLER

MISSY COTTON

Chapter 1

Sharee Miller was a gorgeous, single mother-of-three when she met her husband Bruce Miller. At the time, she was in her early twenties, broke, and weeks away from being homeless.

The couple initially met when Sharee began working at Bruce's automobile scrap yard as a bookkeeper. After only three months, Sharee moved herself and her three kids into Bruce's house and they quickly became a family. Bruce gave Sharee a sense of stability she had never experienced and Sharee was kind, caring, and loving to Bruce.

After only a few more months, the couple married. Domestic bliss loomed on the horizon.

But six months later, Bruce was dead.

Initially, the events that led to Bruce's death were a complete mystery to police until a former homicide detective miles away shot himself in the head and left behind a briefcase of evidence.

How these two deaths were connected would shock police, and lead to one of the most infamous crimes in America.

Chapter 2

Sharee Miller, then Sharee Kitley, was born on October 13, 1971, in Flint, Michigan.

At the time, Flint was a powerhouse of economic growth largely due to the GM Buick and Chevrolet factories that operated in the city. General Motor's history was largely intertwined with Flint—the company's founder had formed the GM company in Flint in 1908. The

GM factories in Flint were also the setting of the and iconic 1936-37 Sit-Down Strike—the strike that led to the creation of the United Auto Worker's union.

Flint made money because Flint made cars.

However, the Kitley family did not drink from the city's pool of wealth. They lived on the town's outskirts, a rough working-class neighborhood. They're home was a single-wide trailer smack-dab in the center of a tornado's playground. Sharee was an only child, she was the sole receiver of her parent's attention, but this attention was not desired by Sharee. Sharee's parents fought often, and when they were finished fighting with each other, they'd fight with Sharee.

In mid 80's, when Sharee was in her early teens, GM Motors closed its factories' doors in Flint. The city quickly fell to pieces, ramshackle remains of the auto empire it had once been. The city fell into a deep depression.

As she watched her hometown descend into ruins, Sharee decided to leave her toxic home for good. At the age of 16, Sharee moved in with her boyfriend at the time, and when that ended she couched surfed and work a variety of dead-end jobs, most of which only lasted a few months.

When she was 18, Sharee found herself pregnant and married to an abusive husband. The two shared a home in yet another low-income project in another rough neighborhood left in the dust of Flint's ruined automobile empire. Sharee watched her childhood repeat itself in front of her own eyes, but this time, it was her first-born son who held the starring role of the helpless child. Sharee ended the marriage after she caught her spouse physically abusing the young boy. It was one of the only lines Sharee drew in the sand—you did not harm her children.

Although Sharee took this brave step towards saving her son, history often repeated itself throughout her life. Two more failed attempts at finding a soulmate yielded two more children for the young woman. The single mother-of-three now resorted to frequently moving from low-income house to low-income house and took any odd job she could find—anything to keep her kids off the street.

Chapter 3

In 1997, Sharee was a single mother-of-three who was three breaths and an electricity bill away from being homeless. During an attempt to keep her kids safe and housed, Sharee took a job as a bookkeeper with B&D Auto, a small auto scrapyard that fit right in in the middle of Flint's automobile history.

Sharee had been hired despite having little-to-no experience keeping books in the past. She had convinced the boss, Bruce Miller, that she was hard-working, a fast learner, and desperate for a paycheque. And that seemed to be enough. That and the fact that Sharee was a stunner. Her bright blonde hair only drew more attention to her enrapturing icy blue eyes.

Bruce was a kind and generous soul. He took a chance on Sharee and it seemed to pay off. Only a few months after Sharee had begun working at the scrapyard, she and Bruce moved their relationship from the office to the bedroom. It wasn't long before Sharee and her three kids moved in with Bruce. The four now lived in a stable, secure home for the first time in any of their lives.

Bruce and Sharee married only months after they first met. Bruce, who has twenty-one his new bride's senior, thought he had finally found the perfect wife. Young, sexy, and loving. It was all he had ever wanted.

Her new life with Bruce was also a dream come true for Sharee. She had finally found a man that treated her right, and in him, she also found security. Ten years ago, she had left her own unhappy parents and embarked on a life of poverty and abuse. Now, she was sitting in the living room of a big house, watching her children—the true loves of her life—swimming in Bruce's above-ground pool. It was the idyllic life she never thought she could have.

But idyllicism did not suit Sharee.

Chapter 4

While Sharee lived the life she had always wanted for herself and her kids, Bruce's own family began to have doubts behind Sharee's motives.

Initially, Bruce's family took no issue with the fact that Bruce's wife was so young. The couple looked so happy and in love, they formed a perfect family. Bruce was even in the process of adopting Sharee's three boys. But things slowly began to change.

Sharee began to take advantage of her new wealth. She no longer worked at the scrapyard but began selling Mary Kay Cosmetics to other bored housewives instead. She began spending every penny of her earnings, and a whole lot more of Bruce's, on luxuries she had never been presented with before. She bought expensive jewelry and clothes, she got her first credit card plus a few more, and she bought an expensive computer for the home.

Bruce, however, did not partake in his family's worries. He was as happy as ever the day Jerry Cassaday stepped into his office and shot him square in the chest. Bruce understood Sharee's desire to buy things, he enjoyed watching her be careless with money for the first time in her life. And most of all, Bruce was proud that she began selling cosmetics door-to-door. An entrepreneur himself, he found Sharee's new profession to be ambitious. Bold. He had no qualms when Sharee brought home expensive dress after expensive dress, and he was nothing but proud when she showed him the computer she claimed was to help her keep track of all her sales.

If you had asked Bruce, he would have said the couple was as happy as could be.

Sharee, evidently, was not happy. Although she was pleased with the security her marriage to Bruce brought, she was bored. She was living the life of a housewife and simply got restless. She started going online and frequenting chat rooms where she could talk to strangers and meet new men. She could talk to these new men and Bruce would be none the wiser.

It was the perfect situation for Sharee. She got to keep the stable home life she knew she needed while engaging in the excitement of meeting new singles and falling in love without the latter threatening the first. In short, she got to have her cake and eat it too.

But this quickly fell apart. Soon, the satisfaction Sharee got from speaking to these men online began to fade. She needed more. She wanted to meet these men, feel their touch. This yearning was fresh in her mind the day she met Jerry Cassaday.

Chapter 5

Jerry Cassaday was working as a pit boss in a Reno casino. Before that, he had been a homicide detective and police officer for the Marshall Police Department and the Cass County Sheriff's Department. He began frequenting online chat rooms after his wife left him. He was lonely and had always wanted a family. He went online hoping to find companionship and an honest connection with a beautiful woman. Instead, he found Sharee Miller.

The two hit it off immediately. For Cassaday, it was love at first sight. He was enraptured by the blue-eyed blonde-haired twenty-something-year-old. There was only one problem: Sharee lived in Flint, Michigan and Cassaday was stuck in Reno, Nevada. They had no way to meet without arousing the suspicions of Sharee's husband Bruce until the perfect opportunity arose—a Mary Kay Cosmetics conference was announced. The location? None other than Reno, Nevada.

Sharee jumped at this opportunity to meet Cassaday in person and the spark they had struck up online burst into flames when they met in person. The two spent every free minute they had together, and Sharee even accompanied Cassaday to work. She would sit at his table and play hands of blackjack. When Cassaday finished for the night, the two would go back to Sharee's hotel room.

While Sharee was honest about being married at the time, she altered many details about her life in Flint to her favor. It was all part of the fantasy she had built up for herself online. Sharee told Cassaday that her husband was a high-ranking member of the mafia who frequently beat her and mistreated her children. They weren't in love, she was just too afraid to leave. Cassaday, who was in his mid 30's at the time, had always wanted a family and was aghast when Sharee told him the details about how her current husband treated herself and her kids. Little did he know it was all a lie.

The picture Sharee painted of her husband Bruce was so far away from the handsome, family-orientated business man that he really was. She wasn't describing reality, she was describing a fantasy. And Cassaday had bought it.

After Sharee inevitably left her new lover behind to return home to Flint, Sharee kept up their flame by sending numerous naked photos by email to Cassaday. They kept in constant touch through emails and instant messages. The two kept in touch so frequently that members of Bruce's family could later recall him complaining about the amount of time Sharee began to spend on her new computer. He knew something was up, he just wasn't sure what.

Sharee continued to build on the fantasy she had created with Cassaday. As well as nude photos, she would send him photos of herself covered in bruise-coloured makeup claiming they were from Bruce. On one special occasion, she went old school and snail-mailed Cassaday a tape labeled For Jerry's Eyes Only...

As Sharee fell deeper into the rabbit hole she had dug, two things became clear to her: the first, Cassaday was completely and utterly under her control, the second, she liked her new fantasy more than her real marriage.

Chapter 6

Sharee Miller's life had taken such a turn from her younger years. She had a stable life, a happy home, and a loving husband. But somehow, this was no longer enough for Sharee. Addicted to the danger of the unknown, Sharee had become bored in her easy marriage. She craved more.

She found the perfect path out of her marriage in Jerry Cassaday. Initially, the thrill of an affair was enough for her, but this eventually grew old—especially when her affair became online only.

Usually, when someone grows tired of their online relationship, they break up with their partner and cease communications. This was not the case with Sharee and Jerry Cassaday. When Sharee grew tired of her online affair with Cassaday she did not stop communications—she increased them. Although she had fallen out of love with the ex-homicide detective, she still needed him for one very specific purpose. He was going to kill her husband for her.

Cassaday had fallen madly in love with Sharee. He believed she was married to an abusive husband who has a high-ranking mafia player. He feared for his beautiful girlfriend and would do almost anything to protect her. Almost wasn't good enough for Sharee though. Sharee was going to use Cassaday to get out of her marriage, and to do so, she was going to have to make him mad first. Mad enough to kill.

Sharee's plan seemed foolproof. Bruce, her husband, was alone at his auto scrapyard a lot, and he always carried a large amount of cash on him, roughly $2000, in order to make change for his customers. Sharee saw this as the perfect opportunity. Someone could easily kill Bruce at his work with no witnesses, and better yet, if they took the cash on him, it would look like a robbery-gone-wrong. This would inevitably point police away from herself. All she needed was someone to pull the trigger.

Chapter 7

At some point during their online relationship, Sharee realized that she had Cassaday wrapped around her finger. She had seduced him in online and in-person and had maintained this enrapturement through sending him endless emails and seductive videos. Sharee began to use this power she had over Cassaday to make him angry. She had already painted her kind, gentle husband to be an abusive mafia man, but she needed more.

About a month after meeting with Cassaday in person, Sharee went to her local pharmacy and purchased a pregnancy test. She knew she wasn't pregnant—she had had her tubes tied after the birth of her third son—but she needed Cassaday to think she was. She went home, took photos of herself with her stomach pushed out, and sent them to Cassaday along with photos of the pregnancy test, which she had drawn lines on so it appeared to be a positive test. To make the lie seem more real, she also sent an image of her third child's sonograms.

I'm pregnant, she wrote Cassaday, with your first children. Twins.

A few weeks later, Sharee sent Cassaday more pictures of her stomach. This time, however, she coated her belly in blue and purple makeup first.

He killed our beautiful babies was the message sent along with the photos.

Cassaday was devastated, his lover's abusive husband had just taken from the world what he thought would be his opportunity to have a normal life with the woman he loved. He fell into a severe state of depression. Cassaday could not take the news. He could no longer watch the woman he loved destroyed by her own oppressive husband. No. He was coming to town to free Sharee and finally have the family he'd always wanted.

Sharee was ecstatic. Through one later-debated series of instant messages, Sharee slowly revealed her perfect plan on how Cassaday should murder Bruce. The whole of Sharee's plan was summed up in only a few damning sentences.

I'll call Bruce at 5pm and tell him to call me when he's leaving. Pull up to the left side of the building, right to the door. He'll be at the desk inside. Take his wallet. Take the whole thing.

Chapter 8

On November 8, 1999, Jerry Cassaday drove from Reno to Flint to kill the man he thought killed his twin babies and repeatedly beat the love of his life.

He followed Sharee's instructions to the word. At 5pm he pulled up to Bruce Miller's auto scrapyard, went inside, shot Bruce in the chest, and took Bruce's wallet. Bruce was on the phone with Sharee at the time, just as she had planned. Sharee had chosen to listen to her husband die.

Cassaday's experience as a homicide detective meant that he could commit the crime without leaving forensic evidence behind. He left the scrapyard office without leaving a single finger or footprint and took Bruce's wallet without ripping the pocket, a general characteristic of a rushed robbery. Investigators were also unable to recover any trace fibers or hairs from the scene or Bruce's body.

After committing the crime he had spent the majority of his life solving, Cassaday turned his car around and headed straight back to Nevada.

Chapter 9

A few hours after listening to her lover shoot her husband, Sharee called her brother-in-law Chuck Miller. She frantically told him that Bruce was missing, he hadn't come home for dinner and his work phone wasn't working. She convinced Chuck to drive out to the scrapyard to check on his brother.

When Chuck arrived, he was affronted with a horrible scene—Bruce was laying face down on the ground dead from a gunshot wound to his chest. His telephone receiver was on the ground next to his face. Within an hour, a full team of homicide investigators were on the scene.

Due to the lack of physical evidence at the scene, investigator's initially had little to go on. The main motive appeared to be robbery, just another day in Flint.

Sharee was brought in for questioning but was never suspected by police. She had been at home all day with her children and several friends. They simply wanted to ask her if she had any idea of who would want her husband dead, and Sharee was prepared for this.

Sharee told detectives that one of her former boyfriends John Hutchinson had owed Bruce several thousands of dollars. Bruce and Hutchinson had several arguments about this as well as the tumultuous state of Sharee and Hutchinson's former relationship.

Hutchison unluckily had no solid alibi. He quickly emerged as the key suspect in Bruce's murder.

To make things worse for Hutchinson, he had agreed to take a lie-detector test to prove his innocence, but the examination did not go smoothly. In the middle of the test Hutchinson collapsed and ended up going to the hospital. Not only had he failed the few questions he had been asked, but he was so clearly stressed about the test that he had physical symptoms.

The general feeling amongst investigators was that Hutchinson had killed Bruce, they just couldn't prove it. While his autopsy revealed that Bruce had been shot by a 20 gauge shotgun, Hutchinson did not own this type of gun and investigators failed to find one during a search of his home.

Eventually, much to Sharee's delight, the case went cold. It wasn't until a seemingly unrelated suicide miles away took place before police had any reason to suspect Sharee.

Chapter 10

After he returned to his home in Reno, Jerry Cassaday expected his relationship with Sharee Miller to continue as usual. He believed that they would continue to date long-distance until the murder investigation cooled down. Then, Sharee would begin a new life in Reno with Cassaday.

This, however, was not the case.

Sharee barely contacted Cassaday after the death of her husband. She didn't initiate any conversations and stopped replying to his emails altogether. Cassaday, still deep in the world of lies Sharee had created, began to panic.

A few weeks after killing her husband, Cassaday decided to pay Sharee a visit to make sure she was doing okay. When he arrived at her home in Flint, his world fell apart.

Sharee was at home with her three kids and a new boyfriend.

She had double-crossed Cassaday within weeks of the murder. Cassaday instantly returned to the state of depression he had been in when he believed that Bruce had killed his baby twins-to-be.

Sharee and Cassaday never spoke again, and Sharee had almost entirely forgot about her ex-lover when police started knocking on her door again.

Chapter 11

Seven hundred miles away from Sharee and Flint, in Kansas City, Missouri, Jerry Cassaday was found dead in his home, a gun in his hand, Bible in his lap, shot in the head. Cassaday could not live with the crimes he had committed for love, especially knowing that the love he felt wasn't real. It was too much for him.

Before he killed himself, Cassaday took measures to ensure his death would be connected back to Sharee and Bruce Miller's murder. Next to his body, police found his open briefcase which contained his suicide note addressed to his parents and a printed transcript of extensive instant messaging conversations. Outside in the trash, investigators also found a scandalous video of a young woman dancing naked addressed directly to Jerry.

Police showed clips of this video to Jerry's neighbors in order to identify the woman dancing. Several neighbors were able to identify Jerry's online girlfriend Sharee, who lived in Flint. When Kansas City police called the Flint sheriff's office to get more information about

Sharee, Flint police were astounded. They instantly knew they had been duped by the blonde, beautiful widow.

When she was identified by Kansas City police, Sharee was immediately connected not only to Cassaday's suicide but also back to her ex-husband Bruce's murder. In his suicide note, Cassaday revealed that he had been the one to kill Bruce. Sadly, it was evident that he still believed many of the lies Sharee had told him. He stated in his note that he had to do it, Bruce had killed his children and that was something he couldn't let go. Even if it meant destroying his own life in the process.

He also described Sharee's role in the murder plot. He stated that she had encouraged him to commit the murder and helped him plan it. He could not have done it without her help. And he had provided investigators with the transcripts to prove it.

Sharee miller was brought in for questioning where she claimed she did not even know Jerry Cassaday. She stuck to this story until police revealed that they had the tape of her dancing, addressed in her handwriting as being For Jerry's Eyes Only. After this, she was forced to change her story. It was undisputable evidence that they had had a relationship.

Sharee then told police she had met Jerry in a computer chatroom while just messing around, trying to figure out something new to do. Computer forensic experts then confiscated both Sharee and Cassaday's computers. What they found inside answered some important questions but raised many others.

Investigators easily found their way into Sharee and Cassaday's private online conversations. They found incriminating evidence on Jerry's computer—the online copy of the instant messaging conversation in which Cassaday and Sharee discussed Bruce's murder. When they confronted Sharee with these messages, she had a planned response: Cassaday was framing her.

Sharee told investigators that in the triangle of herself, her ex-husband Bruce, and Jerry Cassaday, Cassaday was the scorned lover. After she got bored with her online affair, she tried to cut contact with Cassaday, but he wouldn't let her. She claimed that Cassaday had forged the messages to implicate her in something she had never been apart of. Investigators thought that this claim was far-fetched, so they reached out to AOL, the company that hosted the instant messaging service Cassaday and Sharee used to communicate. Surprisingly, AOL took Sharee's side on the issue—it was possible for the messages to have been forged.

Investigators were now tasked with proving the legitimacy of the instant messages that showed Sharee had helped plan Bruce's murder with Cassaday. Under court order, AOL released information about Sharee and Jerry's computer activity. They confirmed that both Jerry and Sharee had been online and logged into the AOL service the same day at the same time for the same length of time as the instant message indicated. Police also found handwritten notes copied in Sharee's writing that listed information found in the messages. If they had been forged, Sharee would not have known this information in order to write it down.

Sharee was now trapped. Although she continued to maintain her innocence, investigators continued to find more and more damning evidence against Sharee.

Sharee had taken steps to cover her online footprints. A day and a half after the death of her husband she had called AOL to change her first name, last name, and her address. After she learned of the suicide of Jerry Cassaday, she did the same thing again. She was clearly worried about the content of her online messages being traced back to her.

Once investigators had confirmed the legitimacy of the messages, they were able to read the diary of Sharee's relationship with Cassaday. They were able to see how she was able to bring Cassaday to a boil, both sexually and emotionally. She brought him into her world the way she wanted him to see it.

Sharee had used her body, in so many ways, to intrigue, seduce, and trap the ex-homicide detective. The only thing that brought her down in the end was Cassaday's conscience on his dying day.

Further, Sharee's actions after her husband's death provided a possible motive for Bruce's murder other than Sharee's freedom. Money.

While Sharee had been loose with money during her marriage, she had gone over-the-top after her husband's death. She used Bruce's life insurance money to dramatically renovate her new inherited home within weeks of his death. She bought herself a new car and spent thousands of dollars on a plethora of items.

When Bruce died, Sharee inherited the family home she had grown so attached to as well as large sums of money both from Bruce's life insurance policy and also from the sale of his auto scrapyard business. Most significantly, though, Sharee had inherited her freedom without having to sacrifice her own and her children's secure, stable life.

Chapter 13

In December, 2000, Sharee went on trial for murder and conspiracy to commit murder.

Throughout the trial, Sharee continued to maintain that the instant messages were forged, as she was innocent of everything. She was simply the victim of an angry lover's broken heart.

The prosecutor's relied heavily on forensic science in their case against Sharee Miller—specifically, on the forensic computer analysis which proved the authenticity of Sharee and Cassaday's messages.

Sharee's trial was a short one. It did not take the prosecutors long to form their case, and the defense presented little-to-no evidence to support Sharee's claims that she was being framed by a dead man.

Sharee was found guilty on the charges of second-degree murder and conspiracy to commit first-degree murder. She was sentenced to life without the possibility of parole.

But this was not the end of Sharee's story.

Chapter 14

In 2009, Sharee Miller was released from prison after serving only nine years of a life without parole sentence. Her release was mandated by a U.S. District Judge who believed that the convicted killer had grounds for a new trial. This was because Jerry Cassaday's suicide note had been presented as damning evidence against Sharee in court despite the fact that Cassaday could not be cross-examined regarding the information in the letter.

Sharee spent a whole three years outside of bars. During this time, she kept a fairly low profile. She stayed in Flint with family, who she spent the most time with. She also spent the three years reconnecting with her sons—the children she spent most of her younger life fighting to support. Sharee's luck finally seemed to be turning in her favor.

But lady luck is fickle. In 2012, Sharee was ordered back to prison by the U.S. Supreme Court. The court disapproved of Sharee's release and mandated that the judge repeals her earlier decision to grant Sharee a new trial. The Supreme Court believed that there was enough additional evidence presented by the prosecutors, with no viable defense to counter it, that the outcome of the trial would have been the same had the suicide note not been presented at all.

Sharee's lawyers told the public that she was simply "disappointed" by her return to prison.

After returning to prison, Sharee and her lawyers quickly filed several appeals targeted at both the decision to return Sharee to court and her original guilty conviction, both of which were lost. Sharee was set to spend the rest of her life in prison for good this time.

That again seemed like the end of Sharee's story until late April 2016.

Seventeen years after manipulating Jerry Cassaday into killing her husband, Sharee Miller admitted her involvement in the crime for the first time through a letter addressed to a County Judge.

In this letter, Sharee claimed that she got caught up in the fantasy world she created with Cassaday. She like being the victim. It was more exciting to her than her real, stable life. However, she quickly found herself in too deep. She had created a monster and the only real way she saw of getting out was through the murder.

If Bruce were to die, neither he nor his family would ever have to discover what she was doing behind his back.

Sharee stated in her confessional letter that she did not enjoy watching her husband die. She wrote, "I had sixteen and a half hours to stop it. And I didn't. I knew it was going to happen and I allowed it. I allowed a man to kill another man based on my lies and manipulation."

She also used her letter as an opportunity to publicly recant the horrible image she had painted of her husband through her messages with Cassaday. She confirmed that Bruce was nothing but a wonderful husband. He had never laid a finger on her, and he always treated herself and her three children with the utmost kindness and respect. She regretted being the reason her children lost such a wonderful father figure—something she had always wanted for them.

While Sharee certainly believed that her confession would put an end to the long-standing controversy surrounding her case, the kind of controversy that inspired both a novel and lifetime movie about her crime, it actually perpetuated a new kind strand of controversy.

To many, especially to Bruce's loved ones, Sharee's confession letter seemed too crafted to be sincere. Sharee was the woman who had manipulated men to kill and die for her all through text. Now, she seemed to be trying to manipulate her way to an earlier release through the same medium.

Whether Sharee will claim another victim as a fool, this time a court judge, is yet to be seen.

SHE KILLED THE PREACHER

John Fontaine

The Case of Mary Winkler

Mary Winkler, at first appearances, would seem to be an altogether normal woman. So too did her family, with a husband who was a Church minister and three young children, girls aged just eight, six and one.

The family lived in Selmer, Tenn., a small town occupied by around 4,500 people, according to the 2015 census. The town is situated to the south west of the state. Not much has happened in Selmer; the most famous person to have been born there was Chad Harville, former pitcher for the Oakland A's, and for one year, the Red Sox. He achieved a 4-9 win-loss record over his career in the MLB.

Today, the most famous- or infamous- person to have come from Selmer is Mary Winkler. In 2006, Mary sparked a border-crossing manhunt, and a court case followed nationwide. She had killed her husband with a shot to the back from the family's shotgun. But it was the gripping, and at times bizarre, court case which gripped the attention of the nation.

Matthew dead, Mary and the family Missing

The date was March 6th, 2007. It was a Tuesday like any other. Mary and Matthew were at home all day together, although Matthew was due to give a sermon that evening.

It was actually members of Matthew's congregation who found his body that night. They had visited his home to check up on him after he had missed the service he was set to give; instead, they found him lying dead, having been shot in the back.

There was no sign of Mary or any of their children at the home, and as such, they were reported missing. The authorities quickly sent out an Amber Alert, since nobody had any idea what could have happened to them, or where they might be. Family and friends had no information to provide police on their whereabouts.

There was every chance that the family had been kidnapped or murdered, and their bodies disposed of elsewhere, although police could not identify a break in, and had no reason to believe that anything of value had been stolen.

It was only a day later that she was arrested in Alabama, having run from the family home with her young children. They were found 350 miles away from home, at Orange Beach, and in the back seat of the van was the family's shotgun. It was certainly suspicious; but what reason could Mary have possibly had for committing such a crime?

The Trial

In the build up to the case going to trial, public interest ramped up. Speculation had been rife about why Mary would have murdered her husband, a seemingly nice, well respected member of the local community. Perhaps either one of them had had an affair, and Matthew had been killed in a crime of passion. Or maybe he had been killed for an insurance claim?

As such, the press reported every step of the story as it came out during the hearing. The trial began when a Tennessee Bureau of Investigation Agent John Mehr read a statement that Mary had made very soon after her arrest. In it, Mary claimed that the couple had been arguing about their family finances, before Mary had shot her husband with their 12 gauge shotgun. She had said that the last thing she had wanted was to actually murder her husband, but she had been brandishing the gun in an effort to convince him to work through their problems, together. The argument had been ongoing throughout the day, and Mary had finally snapped, resorting to drastic measures to be able to convince him. She had never intended to kill him: she had said in the statement, 'I don't want this at all. I don't want any of this to be, at all.'

The statement continued on, and Mary claimed that they had argued often and argued fiercely. 'He had really been on me lately,' Mary had said, 'criticizing me for things- the way I walk, I eat, everything. It was just building up to a point. I was tired of it. I guess I got to a point and snapped.'

At first glance, it would seem that Mary had simply lost her composure, become angry, and killed her husband 'as the red mist had descended'. But after their initial statement, Mary's attorney indicated that there was much more that would come out about Matthew's behaviour when she testified which would help to explain her actions. Clearly, there were more problems with their marriage than the occasional, albeit fierce, argument.

Mary's Crime

The case for the prosecution wasted no time in painting Mary as a cold blooded killer, who left her husband to die without remorse. Admittedly, the plain facts of the case made Mary seem unbelievably guilty. The prosecution relied on several of these facts in their attempt to convince the jury of Mary's guilt for the charge of murder.

Mary had disconnected the phone immediately after she shot her husband, stopping him from being able to call the emergency services, or receive any calls that may have come in. This suggested that Mary had been in full control of her actions, not panicking, since it is unlikely that somebody in a state of anxiety would think to disconnect the phone.

The fact that Mary had attempted to flee to Orange Beach, Alabama, was also a key point for the prosecution. Immediately after Matthew's death, Mary had taken the family minivan to the beach, with her three children. Later on in her defence, Mary would claim that she ran because '[n]obody would believe me, and they'd take the girls away and put me away.' Certainly, in many murder cases, the fact that the defendant flees the scene is a certain indicator of guilt.

The family's daughter Patricia testified that she couldn't understand her mother's actions. All that she knew was that she had heard a 'big boom', and the sound of something heavy hitting the floor. She quickly ran to the bedroom to see her father on the floor, and her mother holding the shotgun. She had no idea what could possibly have provoked her mother to shoot him.

Another sticking point was that the family finances had been 'in shambles' just before the murder had taken place. This had led Mary to become embroiled in what is called a 'check kiting' scam. In it, she had received checks from unidentified accounts in Canada and Nigeria, and had ultimately fallen to a financial scam that had lost the family money. Prosecutors claimed that this could have somehow instigated the argument that led to Matthew's death, and that Mary had felt as if she had no way out of the scam.

They also jumped on the fact that in an initial conversation with investigators, Mary had told them that their marriage was a happy one, and that '[t]here's no poor me. I'm in control.' They clearly wanted to paint a picture of Mary as remorseless, deceitful, and smarter than she looked.

The Cross-examination

During her cross-examination in court, Mary stated that she didn't remember grabbing the gun from the closet in which it was kept. What she did remember was that 'something went off', 'hearing a loud boom', and that 'it wasn't as loud as I thought it would be.' She did admit that she had shot her husband. Matthew rolled from the bed- upon which he had been lying as they had argued- and dropped to the floor. Mary described smelling gunpowder.

Prosecutor Walter Freeland asked her whether she understood that 'pulling a trigger is what makes it go boom', to which she replied that she did.

Matthew asked her why she had snapped and shot him. She could only say 'I'm sorry.' The shotgun blast had been inflicted from behind, directly into Matthew's back, and had caused severe damage to his organs and spine. According to prosecutors, he had in fact still been alive as Mary had run from the house.

But these simple facts were far from the end of the story, as Mary was to reveal.

Appearances and Revelations

At first, Mary spoke of her husband not in the past tense, but in the present, as if she couldn't quite understand how final her actions really had been. In reminiscing about happier times, Mary told the court that her husband was an intelligent, social man, and that the family had shared many 'good times' together. She also seemed to enjoy talking about her children, and the happiness they brought her.

This happy family life, however, was simply one side of the marriage. Mary's attorney stated that '[w]hat went on behind their closed doors is going to have to be told … Some of what we've got from the state of Tennessee touches on sexual abuse.' Their defence was that Matthew had made Mary's life a 'living hell': '[w]e will show you proof that he would destroy objects that she loved, he would isolate her from her family and he would abuse her not just verbally, not just emotional and not just physically—in other ways, too.'

Just before the murder, Mary claimed that Matthew had been threatening their children and even attempted to throttle their infant daughter, Breanna. He had been shouting, angry, because he had wanted a son. As the case went on, it became obvious that this was only the tip of the iceberg, however, and more and more sordid details of their home life would come to light.

Matthew, Mary claimed, was a violent, abusive husband. Shortly after their marriage, he ordered her to stop socialising with any of her family and friends (a common tactic among abusive spouses in order to further isolate their partners from potential help). Winkler's sisters described how Mary seemed stuck in her marriage, unhappy, but unable to leave. In an interview, they said that 'As the years went on, she seemed to be nervous to show love towards us.'

Mary was commonly 'screamed and hollered' at by her husband. 'He just flailed. He's a big guy and he was just all over … He'd point his finger inches away from my nose. Whatever he was upset about, it was my fault,' Mary had said. It could be over anything: 'I was fat, my hair wasn't right, the girls, if something went wrong, it was my fault. I didn't know when it was coming.' Mary described her situation as one familiar to abused wives and husbands across America.

Her attorney, Steve Farese, provided further information based on his conversations with Mary. She had needed her husband's permission for everything, even for getting her hair cut. 'This was constant, and she lived a life where she walked on eggshells.' This abuse, he said, had given Mary symptoms of post traumatic stress disorder, simply because 'she didn't know what was going to happen next.' Furthermore, a psychologist testified as part of Mary's defence, saying that her symptoms were those of clinical depression and PTSD.

During her time on the stand, Mary also claimed that Matthew had forced her to watch pornography with him, and that he had bought her several 'slutty' costumes for sex, which she normally would never have worn, but for fear of her husband. If she refused, Matthew wouldn't hesitate to get physical, hitting her or even using his belt to whip her. Mary famously produced a wig and a pair of white high heels in the witness box during her cross-examination to show the court evidence of Matthew's other side.

Mary stated that she was never happy watching pornography, dressing up in sexy outfits or performing the sex acts that Matthew wanted. She went along with his ideas, however, because she didn't dare face his reaction if she didn't. 'I'd just do anything to help him stay happy.' Throughout these revelations, Mary was visibly embarrassed and uncomfortable. Clearly she would have preferred that none of them had ever come to light; but Mary felt it necessary to brave what her neighbors, and the nation, might think in order to clear her name and justify her actions.

Mary's family had been quick to corroborate her side of the story. Her father, Clark Freeman, had spoken out through Good Morning America and detailed the 'physical, mental, verbal' abuse that his daughter had suffered. Other friends came forward during the court case, and gave similar verdicts on their relationship. A friend of Mary's,

Rudie Thomsen, said that '[o]ne Sunday, Mary came into the church and I looked at her and she had a black eye.' Similarly, Mary's friend Amy Redmon agreed that Matthew had been controlling: '[h]e was an authority figure, and he made the decisions basically. It was obvious.'

Conversely, Matthew's family denied that their son had been anything like Mary had depicted in her defence testimony. Matthew's father, Charles Daniel Winkler, said that his son was a kind, gentle man, who could have done nothing to justify what the defence was claiming. Diane spoke several times during the trial, lashing out at Mary: 'You've never told your girls you're sorry! Don't you think you at least owe them that?'

The dramatic story of a supposedly kindly, gentle church minister having such a sordid, cruel and abusive hidden life gripped America. The case was covered extensively on all major networks, discussed on late night panel shows

The Jury's Verdict

While the prosecutors had tried to convince the jury to convict her on a charge of first degree murder, they were unsuccessful. The jury came to their verdict by April, that year. It took them eight hours to deliberate their way to the decision; this mirrored the response of the nation, which was similarly undecided on just what punishment Mary really deserved.

Mary was found guilty of voluntary manslaughter, a charge which carries a far more lenient sentence than murder. While murderers can receive full life sentences, and in certain states receive the death penalty, the maximum sentence for voluntary manslaughter is only 6 years.

Mary showed little emotion at the verdict, but did embrace each of her relatives afterwards. In a show of support, her family had been sat in the row behind her, and all linked arms with one another to demonstrate their solidarity. Afterwards, she was taken back into custody to await sentencing.

Mary's attorney stated afterwards that Mary's testimony had been central in securing the more lenient sentence. 'I think Mary's testimony was integral in this decision. They had to hear it from Mary', Farese told the press. 'They judged her credibility and they saw that she had an abusive relationship and they made their judgment based upon that.'

For Mary, the most important implication of the verdict was that she could finally begin to think of being reunited with her children. Speaking on her behalf after the trial, Farese continued: 'We would like to do so many things to open up communication between Mary and the paternal grandparents and to get the children out of this cycle of constant upheaval over this terrible tragic event.' But the question of how long she would be in prison remained.

Mary's sentencing was scheduled for May 18th, at which point both Mary and the prosecution would have a final chance to address the court before the judge decided on the final jail term. However, the situation looked positive for Mary. Not only would the five months that she had been imprisoned awaiting trial be taken into consideration, but the judge had indicated that alternatives to incarceration would be on the table. Perhaps Mary could avoid jail time altogether.

Sentencing: The Trial at an End

Due to a scheduling error, the hearing took place around three weeks late, on June 8th.

Mary took to the stand one last time to plead for mercy. She read aloud from a prepared statement, telling Matthew's family of her sorrow and remorse for her actions. She was 'so sorry that this had happened', and would 'always miss and love' her husband. 'I ask for mercy and understanding, but I know whatever decision you reach today will be right ... I ask you to please let me go home today and be with my children.' Tabitha Freeman- Mary's sister- had also pleaded for leniency, in particular to let Mary be reunited with her children. She went as far as calling Mary 'the best example of a good person I can think of'.

Members of Matthew's family, too, took to the stand to plead their case for the prosecution. Charles and his wife were clearly hurt and in disbelief at Mary's actions both in murdering their son, and believed that Mary had purposefully smeared his name at trial. 'The monster that you have painted for the world to see? I don't think that monster existed,' Diane Winkler had said.

After speaking their pieces, all that Mary, her family, and Matthew's parents could do was wait until the judge's decision. The trial- as well as the very public 'trial' that Mary had been through in the media- was finally at an end.

The defence had requested that Mary be granted full probation, or judicial diversion, both outcomes which would have meant that Mary would spent no further time in prison, and even that her record would be cleared of wrongdoing altogether. This request was denied.

After recess, Mary was told that she would spend 3 years in prison for her crime. But Circuit Judge J. Weber McCraw reduced that amount to just 210 days total in prison before she would be allowed to leave on probation. She also had that sentence reduced further, due to the fact that she had spent five months incarcerated waiting for trial.

Moreover, that time would be spent not in jail, but in a mental health centre in Tennessee. There, she would receive treatment for both her depression and post traumatic stress disorder. After such a long ordeal, with the prosecution fighting to either put Mary on death row or to imprison her indefinitely, it seemed that she had gotten off with hardly a slap on the wrist.

Steve Farese branded the sentence 'a victory': '[s]he could be in prison for life, and that's what everybody thought she was headed for to begin with.' Her other attorney, Leslie Ballin, said '[s]he'll be able to get out and fight the battle she wants to, and that is to get her children back.' Mary could finally think about the future again.

But certain signs indicated that it would not be as easy to reconcile with her children and family as she might hope. Matthew's family left the courtroom without making a comment to the press, as did the prosecution, clearly disappointed in the verdict. They gave no indication that they would be happy to open dialogue about Mary's daughters- not with the woman whom they believed to have murdered their son in cold blood.

The aftermath of Mary's release

Mary was released on August 14th, 2007. She had only been sentenced the previous June.

Upon her release, her lawyer informed the press that Mary would not be speaking with them, to maintain her privacy. During her time in the mental health facility, Mary could finally begin her attempt to win full custody of her three daughters, and she was still fighting this case at the time of her release. She had not seen her children, apart from Patricia's brief testimony as part of the case, for over a year. Throughout the case, and after Mary's release, her children were staying with Matthew's family.

Moreover, she was still fighting a $2 million dollar civil lawsuit filed by Matthew's parents. They also took legal measures, which, if successful, would have meant that the custody of Mary's children remained with them.

After her release, Mary seemed happier to her family and friends. From an outside perspective, it could be easy to claim that this was just as much due to her happiness at avoiding a jail sentence as it was to her being rid of an abuser. She was in fact living with friends at first after her release, and went back to work at a dry cleaners in McMinnville, Tenn., 200 miles from Selmer.

In the same interview as was mentioned before, Mary's sisters agreed that she had changed entirely. After years of shyness, Mary seeming unable or unwilling to show love to them for fear of her husband's violence, she seemed to finally be able to open up. 'Now it's back to the old Mary [who] loves us and doesn't care to come and hug us and gives us a kiss on the cheek.'

Since then, Mary lived in McMinnville. She has moved between jobs, working at the dry cleaners, before starting work at a nursery. She briefly dated the brother of one of her most vocal supporters, Paul Pillow; afterwards, she moved in with Wayne Cantrell, a preacher living in Smithville nearby.

Mary regained custody of her three children in 2008, but by 2010, received the news that she had multiple sclerosis. Her diagnosis came at the worst time, as she was settling down in her new life; she had not long started medical school with the desire to become a nurse, and had to quit since the work would be too demanding. She hasn't returned to work since.

One comfort for Mary was that Matthew's parents seemed close to being able to forgive her. After her diagnosis, they gave Mary some time off from parenting by taking care of the children for a weekend, which soon turned into several months. Daniel Winkler has preached several times since the events on the topic of forgiveness, although when asked by local press why he chose the topic, he has refused to answer, presumably preferring to keep those details private.

Mary, too, preferred to put the past behind her. In an interview with WAFF 48, the NBC affiliate in Huntsville AL., she stated how she would prefer to stay out of the limelight, particularly for the sake of her girls. 'Whatever reason people have any problem with me, that's fine. Everybody's entitled to their opinion, but these girls are treated for who they are, not because of what their mother's done ... They're three very fine young ladies'.

Concluding Thoughts

Some members of the public reacted with disgust at the abnormally short sentence that Mary was given, and questioned whether a husband would have been given the same leniency as Mary was. Men's rights activist Glenn Sacks publicly questioned whether a man would have been shown such leniency, and pointed to the case of Scott Peterson (who received the death penalty for the murder of his pregnant wife) to indicate that no, a man would not. He also argued that the idea of abuse had been widened to include simple criticism, and should therefore not necessarily be used as defence of murder.

Conversely, there have been many women put in prison for murdering their abusive husbands, some for much longer than Mary Winkler. The 'battered woman defense', or the preferred terminology today of 'battering and its effects', is not a genuine legal defence in itself; it can, however, be used to convince a court of diminished responsibility. Its effectiveness is due to the sympathy that it elicits from jurors, who can be convinced that abuse is a form of provocation, and the murder a form of self defense. Under this defense, Mary's short sentence makes sense.

The case has remained a touch stone with regards to spousal abuse in the U.S. A made-for-TV movie, 'The Pastor's Wife', was released in 2011. It was based on the book of the same title, written by Dianne Fanning, an award winning crime writer. The story was changed somewhat, with the inclusion of a financial subplot involving tax fraud. However, it also made use of real life interviews with people who knew the Winklers- including Matthew's parents. His mother revealed that she could never believe Mary's story. Charles admitted that Mary's story could be true, and that he could forgive her if she confessed her purposeful intention to murder Matthew.

As for the community in which the family had lived, the reaction was largely one of forgiveness. According to members of that community, the town's 'Christian roots and ... its tendency to give people the benefit of the doubt' meant that they took Mary at her word. Mary's quite life in McMinnville and Smithville similarly shows that the American public would rather leave her and her family alone after their painful ordeal.

HICCUP GIRL : THE TRUE STORY OF JENNIFER MEE

122

SAMANTHA RYANN

For a resident Floridian, it sounded like your typical Saturday night news report. Another shooting in some dark alley. Nothing extraordinary for a country where there are more guns than people and violence is ripe, shootings occurring on the daily. This is especially the case in Florida, where state firearm laws are considered lenient by national standards and registered gun-owners are free to 'concealed carry' at their home, place of work, or on the road to either.

Another day, another homicide. Unremarkable, considering the circumstances too. In an armed robbery, a gun is bound to go off, if tragically, on an unsuspecting victim. That's the nature of a gun-related crime.

But things get interesting when we consider the details of the crime. The perpetrators were young, almost teenagers, and the alleged orchestrator was only nineteen. Moreover, this wayward teenager had an unusual celebrity past, having been in the public eye before.

Who is this young delinquent? Her name is Jennifer Mee, and before she became embroiled in a money-making scheme with two wannabe thugs, the world simply knew her as "Hiccup Girl."

The Curse of the Hiccups

On January 23, 2007, 15-year old Jennifer seemed to have caught a bad case of the hiccups. Though uncomfortable, she assumed, as anyone might, that in time, they would go away on their own. However, when that Tuesday turned into Wednesday, and Wednesday turned into Thursday, the uncomfortable situation turned into a deeply unpleasant condition as the hiccups not only failed to cease, they had grown more frequent and vicious in nature.

The hiccups had intensified to 50 times a minute. Mee and her family were ready to try just about anything to make them stop.

Indeed, there wasn't a home remedy Mee's mother, Rachel Robidoux had not employed on her daughter. From eating mustard to drinking vinegar and swallowing scoops of peanut butter, nothing was too far-fetched a remedy, if it meant easing her daughter's pain.

"I get really bad chest pains, abdominal pains, throat pains, back pains..." Jennifer Mee told an ABC action news anchor in one televised report.

To prevent possible choking and to help keep pain at bay, she was forced to abandon some of her favorite meals, able to only eat soft foods. The uncontrollable spasms also meant Mee couldn't even enjoy a good night's sleep. After many sleepless nights, she had to be medicated to get her rest.

The incessant hiccupping affected her quality of life in other ways too. Like any 15-year-old, the world revolved around school and friendships, but her condition prevented her from participating in both. She was forced to stay home to keep from distracting fellow students and disrupting classroom activities.

The stress was getting to be too much, and despite the efforts of myriad medical specialists, nothing seemed to work. She had passed every conceivable test her doctors had employed, from blood tests to CAT Scans yet remained immune to the effects of any medicine she was prescribed. Desperate, Mee's family turned to the media for help.

In a swift response, the Tampa Bay Times sent a reporter to their home for an interview. The video went viral on their website, and the very next day, Rachel Robidoux said she found herself juggling "30 to 50 calls from the media." Everyone wanted to speak with "the hiccup girl."

So it began. Making one televised appearance after another, Jennifer Mee and her hiccups sprang into the TV sets of her fellow Floridians, before national news stations caught on. Her story spread and she gained celebrity nationwide. Before long, Mee's fame traversed national borders, infecting everywhere from Europe, to the east and Japan, with her story.

At first, it seemed that everyone wanted to help. For over a month, as Mee's condition stubbornly persisted, her family sifted through thousands of email suggestions for folk cures and considered medicines both conventional and homeopathic. Mee even entertained the Hic-Cup, an anti-hiccup device designed to reset the vagus and phrenetic nerves through a "natural electric current," allegedly curing hiccups.

But one appearance on NBC's Today show seemed to turn her quasi-fame into quasi-notoriety, dividing viewers as to the veracity of her condition.

For the segment, Mee and Robidoux were flown into New York to speak with a medical expert, gastroenterologist Dr. Roshini Rajapaksa, about Mee's few remaining options. With news hosts Meredith Vieira and Matt Lauer, Mee was an amusing presence, punctuating her companions' questions, comments and occasional banter with her hiccups.

That is, until she spoke.

When Mee spoke, something curious happened. 'Hiccup girl' would stop hiccupping. Noticing this, Matt Lauer lightheartedly gestured, "So there's the solution right there. Don't stop talking."

But Matt Lauer wasn't the only one that noticed. Following that damning interview, Internet bloggers, many of which had already accused the family of trying to profit off of Mee, started accusing Mee herself of faking her way to fame. Mee and her family found themselves facing an uproar of nasty online comments, and a slew of harassing phone calls.

In school, Mee was teased by kids who thought her hiccups were all part of an act for attention. Some taunts stuck more than others.

"Are you drunk, bitch?" one asked. "You pregnant?"

One after another, students demanded she "Stop faking!" Mee felt more isolated and alienated than ever before.

Classmates weren't the only ones harassing Mee. The family phone rang day and night with media requests for interviews and follow-ups. "Good Morning America," having lost the race to competitor Today, called 57 times in one day to get a scoop on the story they failed to report first.

"Honestly, the best way I can describe it, is that they call it a case of the hiccups, but I call it the curse of the hiccups," Mee's mother said in a telephone interview one afternoon. "It felt like a nightmare."

The nightmare had only just begun.

A Troubled Past

Jennifer Mee's hiccups ceased about five weeks later in early March, after undergoing a combination of treatments including hypnotism and acupuncture. However, her parents claim it was a prescription medication that ultimately relieved Mee of her affliction, a drug used to treat individuals suffering from Tourette Syndrome.

This detail would become critical in her defense against the charge of first-degree murder of Shannon Griffin.

But until then, she could enjoy a return of normalcy. That is, if that's what she had wanted.

According to police reports, just months after her taste of fame, she ran away from home the summer of 2007. In her mother's words, she was found "walking the streets aimlessly." At 17, two years later, she left home for good, thus beginning what Major Mike Kovacsev of St. Petersburg Police Department called "a transient lifestyle."

Speaking with Good Morning America in 2010, he painted a bleak portrait of Jennifer Mee as a young woman. Since she turned 18, he estimated at least "a dozen contacts with her" over the past year alone.

Still, she was never arrested in connection with a crime. Major Kovacsev explained that while her home life seemed precarious, as she "bounced between different apartments and different hotels," he never actually booked her. In fact, "she was never a suspect in any cases, but she was a victim and a subject in several times. And a witness to several crimes," Kovacsev added.

Her MySpace bio seemed to support the implication that she led a troubled life.

"My name is jennifer, im almost 19 but dont let the age fool you, the struggles ive been through has made me grown up so much. Im always havin fun chillin"

However, she did not self-identify as a victim. Posting pictures of herself flashing the finger and sticking out her pierced tongue, friends and contacts came to know her as a bit of a diva, rebellious, and more trouble-seeking than

troubled.

Several friends said that after the media frenzy ended, Mee found attention on the streets, selling drugs, and meeting people online. She allegedly told some friends that she wanted to have a drug-selling empire.

Her online presence seems to emphasize this bad-girl persona. Among her Myspace pictures, she featured her boyfriend's jail booking photo. On Facebook, she heavily implies abuse of drugs and alcohol. And against the backdrop of pink money on that Myspace page, she explicitly describes herself as a "female version of a hustla" living in "St. Pistol" Florida.

According to Ms. Robidoux, her daughter's behavior began to sour after the fame had died down. "I just noticed a big change in her," said Robidoux. "It didn't happen overnight. [But] she wanted to be her own person at a very young age." Mee's father, Chris Robidoux agreed, saying, "This is not the Jennifer I know."

But True Crime novelist M. William Phelps, would later disagree. After conducting extensive research on Mee for his newest book, One Breath Away, he publicly claimed that Mee was troubled prior to her gaining hiccup celebrity.

She came from a poor family – her mother a waitress, her stepfather on benefits – and grew up sharing a bedroom with her four little sisters. With little money to spare, her family eventually moved from pricey Vermont to Florida, but not before she endured daily rapes by two different, unidentified men, for a period of two years. By thirteen, she was on the street, dealing drugs, including crack cocaine, for money.

Her troubles didn't end there. Impregnated by her teenage boyfriend, she suffered regular beatings, including one that caused her to miscarry. From the stomach punches to the humiliation of growing up poor, Mee battled depression and suicidal ideation well before the hiccups came.

And when they did, Mee saw only catastrophe. Believing the hiccups would never stop, she told her mother she didn't think she would ever get married, have kids, or lead a normal life. The incessant teasing from classmates, and online harassment almost pushed her over the edge—literally. Rachel Robidoux listened in horror as Mee declared, "I want to jump off the Sunshine Skyway."

In January of 2010, the year in which her life would change forever, St. Petersburg police again issued a missing person report for Jennifer Mee.

By then, they knew her fairly well. Cops would visit Mee repeatedly to break up fights between her and her boyfriend, aspiring rapper Lamont Newton. In fact, Mee and the company she kept had earned quite the reputation as quarrelsome and disruptive neighbors.

Former landlord Art DeCosmo was forced to kick her out after complaints of "suspicious behavior" from his tenants.

"I asked her to leave on Oct. 1," DeCosmo said. "She just really didn't want to conform. We were getting calls because of loud music, her sitting out front with different people. It appeared they were not doing the right thing."

DeCosmo had taken pity on Mee who paid him with a government disability check, and allowed her to rent out his apartment because Mee's mother had been a former tenant. But something had to give. While Mee "always apologized," a few days later, DeCosmo said he "would get another call from tenants about the loud music."

By then, Jennifer Mee, her boyfriend Lamont Newton, and his best friend, Laron Raiford, were low on cash. The trio started devising a plan to make some money.

The Crime

On October 23, 2010, the three roommates headed out on the town. According to the prosecution, Mee, who had connected with 22-year old Shannon Griffin online, agreed to lure him to an abandoned home where Newton and Raiford would rob him for petty cash.

In what Mee later called a "hazy" state, she messaged him through a social networking site on her phone, saying she wanted to meet and "buy some marijuana." Having not slept for days, and high from a combination of ecstasy, marijuana, and cocaine, she couldn't exactly recall how Shannon Griffin ended up at that abandoned home in the 500 block of Seventh Street N. By the time Griffin was shot, however, Mee claimed she was half a mile away.

Jennifer Charron, who lived with Mee and the two other suspects at the time of the murder, is the only one not charged in connection with the case. Her timeline of events seemed to corroborate Mee's claims.

According to Charron, they were all planning to see the movie Paranormal Activity that evening, but not before her roommates got some money. After they left, it was Mee that came back first, looking panicked and breathing heavily, saying she had heard gunshots. A distraught Raiford followed suit not long after, saying that Newton had been shot. But then a minute later, Newton disproved this, appearing at the door to say that a third man, victim Shannon Griffin had been shot. To Charron, it looked like an escalated altercation between three men. Mee had nothing to do with it.

In her first interview with police, Mee indicated that the shooting had been the result of a love triangle between Mee, Raiford, and Griffin. Her boyfriend Newton, unaware of her sexual relationship with Raiford, was not the triggerman. It was Raiford, his best friend, who couldn't stand the thought of sharing her with a new man.

Though she later changed her story, her defense team said there was compelling evidence that sexual conduct between the three individuals had occurred the night of the murder.

Among the items found at the scene, police collected a condom wrapper with Raiford's DNA on it. Griffin's body was found partially undressed, with his pants pulled down to his ankles. And a relative of Griffin's even testified that Griffin had a date that night, and watched him put on cologne before leaving the house.

Prosecutors Jan Olney and Christopher LaBruzzo dismissed the claim. After all, as prosecutor LaBruzzo pointed out, the condom wrapper could have been left behind after a previous encounter, as there was no way to tell whether it had been produced that day. The simplest explanation was that the two men had robbed Griffin at gunpoint. When he struggled, they shot him with a .38-caliber revolver four times in the chest.

Whether or not the murder had been premeditated, his wallet was found in the trio's apartment, together with its contents—a $50 prize in cash, and his IDs. With

Mee's fingerprint on Griffin's driver's license, the prosecutors argued that there was no way she knew nothing about the robbery plot, nor that this had been a mere crime of passion. Jennifer Mee was the lure in a robbery gone wrong.

The Defense

Though Mee eventually pled "not guilty," her lawyers submitted several plea deals prior to trial. The first asked for a ten-year prison sentence, and the second for fifteen. Prosecutors denied both deals.

With no choice but to proceed with the case, John Trevena presented the facts as he knew them; Jennifer Mee was a victim, not a criminal, and her past, both public and private, is testament to this.

He began by arguing that his client was suffering from schizophrenia and Tourette Syndrome.

Tourette's, a disorder of the nervous system that can cause involuntary repetitive movements and sounds, explained the hiccups that made her notorious, and the Tourette's medication, Thorazine, explains how she kept them at bay all these years.

But Thorazine is frequently used to treat psychotic disorders as well. Is this what kept Mee's schizophrenia from being diagnosed for so long?

Trevena emphasized that his patient was not mentally sound and that her condition affected her decision-making ability at the time of the crime. While "it won't be used as a direct cause for what occurred" Trevena explained, "it might help explain her errors in judgment and her often thoughtless response to law enforcement."

He hoped this would also help explain one damning piece of evidence, a phone call between Mee and her mother, recorded while Mee was in custody and played before the court by the prosecution.

On the tape, Rachel Robidoux asks what happened, and why.

"Because I set everything up" Mee is heard saying, close to tears. "It all went wrong, Mom. It just went downhill."

The judge had ordered Mee to undergo a psychiatric evaluation in order to determine whether she was competent to stand trial. The court psychiatrist considered her competent, but diagnosed her intelligence as "low normal."

The burden of proof, to show that Mee was innocent—merely brainwashed and manipulated by her roommates, a far cry from a thieving murderess—fell heavily on the defense. At the end of the five-day trial, Trevena and his team waited and prayed for a more lenient charge of manslaughter, or accessory to murder.

From 'Hiccup Girl' to 'Hiccup Killer'

The day after Griffin's murder, 19-year old Jennifer Mee was arrested for participating in the murder of Shannon Griffin, a 22-year old Walmart employee she had met online. She had not pulled the trigger, on this point both defense and prosecution agreed. But could she have masterminded the plot? Or was she just an innocent bystander?

Three years later, on September 20, 2013, Jennifer Mee, now 22 herself, sat in the Clearwater courtroom awaiting a verdict. Would she be found guilty of first-degree murder, or guilty of a lesser charge? The evidence seemed mounted against her. The jury returned after just four hours of deliberation.

"We the jury find as follows the defendant in this case guilty of murder in the first degree as charged…"

With the heel of her hand, Jennifer Mee is seen pressing against her teary eyes in an attempt to hold back her emotions, but by the time she is led out of the courtroom, she has burst into mournful sobs. Shortly thereafter, her mother, who had missed the verdict, would walk in to find her daughter in handcuffs, crying hysterically.

Once eager to speak to reporters about her hiccupping daughter, she made no comment now to the news reporters that swarmed around her after the trial.

The mother and daughter were not alone in their pain. As the verdict was read, some jurors themselves fought back tears. Doug Bolden, the victim's cousin, described hearing the verdict as "surreal," after nearly three years of waiting. But he was not rejoicing either.

"It's a victory, but there are no winners," he told reporters.

While Mr. Bolden had lost his cousin for life, Jennifer Mee would serve life, without the possibility of parole, at Lowell Correctional, in Pinellas County. Judge Nancy Moate Ley dutifully handed down the unforgiving sentence, the only possible sentence for such a verdict.

No, she hadn't pulled the trigger. In fact, prosecutors had even admitted that Jennifer Mee was "no mastermind." But according to Florida law, knowingly participating in a felony activity that results in murder is commensurate with personally pulling that trigger.

In other words, it didn't matter that Mee had no intention of committing homicide. Simply because it was the byproduct of a robbery she had intended to commit, she is, under this Florida statue, sufficiently guilty of murder in the first degree.

The statute, among the nation's strictest, is highly controversial for this reason. Mee's defense team argued that she had no idea there would be guns involved, let alone that the plan would end with a fatality. But again, according to the law, this didn't absolve her of guilt.

As a result, Jennifer will likely die in prison. But not just any prison.

She has to cohabit with some of Florida's most violent women in a maximum-security facility, allegedly for her own protection. Due to her amusing celebrity past, she is considered a "high profile inmate."

Jennifer Mee recalls the moment she learned of her newest nickname.

"When I first came on this compound I had a lady tell me, 'Aren't you the Hiccup Killer?' I just looked at her and kept going."

Prison Life

Jennifer Mee sat quietly, looking as she had at fifteen years of age. Described as a model inmate, news anchor Sarina Fazan wanted to learn more about Mee, her past, and her new life, or semblance thereof, behind bars. In the ABC action news exclusive, Mee opened up.

"I got cased up with the wrong crowd of people," she said. "Unfortunately, when I started experimenting with drugs, I just felt like I was invincible to everything."

Like her parents, she blamed her hiccups and the whirlwind media tour for getting to her head, or as she described it in an earlier 2011 interview with the Today show, 'leading her down "the path of the devil.'"

However, Derris Singleton, an acquaintance from middle school, said Mee liked "bad boys" and often texted about getting drunk and high even before hiccup notoriety. "It wasn't being hiccup girl that went to her head," Singleton stated. "It was hanging out with the wrong people."

Even Kayla Ann Labonte, a friend of Mee's who said the two "hung out a lot" in the 10th grade, admitted that she "always hung out with the wrong people." Once she "went national," they lost touch, but she never thought Mee would become so embroiled in a life of crime.

"She was a good friend," Labonte continued. "I just don't know why she would make a stupid choice to do that and throw away her whole life that."

Mee clutches her arms around her waist as she describes her time in Lowell. Some days it is "a nightmare" and others, "it is what it is," she concedes, looking defeated.

After a denied appeal, her attorney says she has less than a 1-2% chance of ever being released. Mee said she keeps her hopes up by remembering she has a family waiting for her at home. For them, she must keep fighting.

Over the years, Jennifer Mee has garnered supporters—or at the very least—sympathizers of her case. One unlikely advocate, Piers Morgan, revealed his feelings after interviewing Mee for the third episode of the ITV series, Killer Women.

"Of all the women I interviewed for this series, Mee was the one for whom I felt most sympathy... Not for the crime she helped perpetrate but for the fact that she had her life turned upside down by freakish chronic hiccups that turned her briefly into a global celebrity... That horrible affliction and subsequent flirtation with fame damaged her schooling and home life – and sent her down a path to undesirable company, petty crime and ultimately a murder... Without the hiccups, she would almost certainly never have strayed into that other, darker life."

He also discussed meeting Mee's mother and siblings.

"My interview with [Mee] was very sad, but my interview with her poor mum and her little sisters was utterly heartbreaking... So many lives wrecked by a moment of dumb madness... Jennifer tried to feign toughness when I met her in prison – but I looked into her eyes and saw a frightened young woman who knew she had destroyed her life and desperately wanted a second chance to prove she's not the evil killer everyone thinks she is."

Morgan said he is troubled by the verdict considering that Mee "never pulled the trigger, wasn't there when it happened and didn't know Shannon would be killed... Jennifer didn't know her two wannabe gangster mates had a gun and thought they were just going to rough this guy up a bit."

Calling the verdict "incredibly draconian" for the circumstances, he noted that such a case was uniquely American. No such sentence would have been handed down in the U.K.

Her long-time sympathizer, New York Times bestselling author M. William Phelps, agrees that the verdict is ultimately unfair.

Over Skype, he tells ABC Action News that "she does not belong in prison for the rest of her life."

But how does Jennifer feel? When asked what sentence would be fair for her, she surprised some viewers.

"At least twenty years," she replied. "Somebody's life was taken, somebody's loved one, somebody's child."

Though Mee may be a victim too, and many certainly consider her one, it is critical we do not forget about the life that was completely extinguished. That somebody's loved one, Shannon Griffin.